Thomas W. Hall

Sun and Earth as Great Forces in Chemistry

Thomas W. Hall

Sun and Earth as Great Forces in Chemistry

ISBN/EAN: 9783742808073

Manufactured in Europe, USA, Canada, Australia, Japa

Cover: Foto ©Thomas Meinert / pixelio.de

Manufactured and distributed by brebook publishing software
(www.brebook.com)

Thomas W. Hall

Sun and Earth as Great Forces in Chemistry

SUN AND EARTH

AS

GREAT FORCES IN CHEMISTRY.

BY

THOMAS W. HALL,

M.D., L.R.C.S.E.

" Latent scintillula forum."

LONDON:

TRÜBNER & CO., 57 & 59 LUDGATE HILL.

1874.

PREFACE.

—o—

I HAVE called this work "Sun and Earth as Great Forces in Chemistry," because I have there viewed the entire of chemical phenomena as heat acting on matter; and where matter and heat are all in all, or are the sole active and passive agents, sun-heat and matter, in all its extent, whether as a minute single chemical or the whole globe, must have influence, and must occupy important positions. I have regarded, accordingly, the sun as our highest chemist, and the earth, as a whole, as but a vast chemical; and have also held that, as the sun, and all other heat sources, can affect matter only through its heat constitution—that is, its conductivity, heat capacities, and mass—these properties of matter come to have, in chemistry, an influence not only fundamental and radical, but that ramifies, without exception, minutely throughout all actions of chemistry. Again, in chemistry, so linked with electricity and heat in a science *par excellence* of transformations, I have thought it imperative to give some prominence to galvanism, to the dynamical theory of heat, and to the subject of matter's form in its correlation to heat. By the introduction, as essentialities, into chemical reasoning of electricity, and of heat, not only of the sun, but of secondary sources and of whatever phase; and also by the help of the study of matter in its molecular forms, and in its vaster extent as seen in the largest of our chemicals, the whole globe; by the aid of matter's heat constitution, by means of form's relationship to latent heat, and by the dynamical theory of heat, I have obtained an adequately solid basis upon which to found an entirely new chemical theory; that is, by the light thrown by all the data above mentioned, I have been able to give some distinct explanation of chemical affinity and attraction, of the elementary forms of chemicals, of the causes, nature, and results of chemical combinations, of combustion, and of decomposition, and also of many phenomena of the galvanic battery and of electricity. While holding the dynamical theory of heat, and doing my best to engraft it on chemistry, I have not scrupled, when convenient, to use the old views and phraseology of heat. Finally, I have seldom anticipated objections, but most humbly deprecate any imputation of dogmatism ; and if such should seem apparent, it must be laid to my earnest endeavour to avoid any prolixity.

PARIS, 1874.

CONTENTS.

PART I.

CHAPTER I.

CHAPTER II.

CHAPTER III.

b

CHAPTER IV.

CHAPTER V.

CHAPTER IX.

CHAPTER X.

PART II.

CHAPTER I.

CHAPTER II.

SUN AND EARTH

AS GREAT FORCES IN NATURE.

—◇—

PART I.

CHAPTER I.

Heat the basis of chemical theory. Heat of all sources and phases.
Equal importance of sun-heat and fire-heat in chemical theory.
There is a fixed quantity of solar heat for the earth : effects of
this. Of sun-got latent heat : its indisputable existence in all
things, and its importance : its universality has made it easy
to be overlooked compared with the more partial fire-got latent
heat. Sun-heat effects to be understood through their analo-
gies with those of fire.

I WILL adopt for the basis for theorising on the
phenomena of chemistry the manifestations of
heat force on matter, called conducted, thermometric, latent, and specific heat ; thus considering
the whole of chemistry as but heat acting on
matter. Heat is therefore highly important to
our views of chemical acts, and we shall have to
begin with it even from its very sources.

A

There are two chief sources of heat in chemistry,
the fire and the sun. Fire is the principal source
of heat for the chemistry of the laboratory and of
the arts, and the sun·for that of nature. Sun
effects and fire effects are therefore, at least, of
equal moment in chemical theory, and must be
equally studied. This, as regards sun effects, has
by no means been adequately done, for chemistry.
is greatly an experimental science, and chemists,
being masters of fire, are able to experiment with
it, and have become well acquainted with its effects
on matter; not having, however, the experimental
command of the sun, chemists have been less
attracted to the study of sun effects on matter,
and have, it is to be feared, undervalued their
importance and neglected them. But although
we cannot study sun effects experimentally, yet
we can do so theoretically to a very useful extent,
by comparing them with those of fire, which we
know, and to which sun effects must in essentials
be alike, for the forces of fire and sun are similar
—namely, heat. Fire, as compared with the sun,
is a near, temporary, partial heat source, the sun
being a distant, everlasting, universal, equable
heat source; and these sun and fire differences
are weighty, for though they do not change the
quality of the force at work, heat, they influence
its quantity, and thus modify its actions. But

here I must at once state that by sun I do not
mean the actual sun himself, or any of his temporary, partial effects. During night the actual
sun is, for part of the globe, absent, and the
sun shines less in winter than summer, and this
produces temporary sun effects like those of fire's;
but, unlike fire's, there is regular, constant repetitions of these varying sun effects, which in the
long-run produce one general, equal, constant sun
effect, to which I allude when I say *our* sun. *Our*
sun therefore stands, in reference to the varying
effects of sun-heat, as climate does to varying
meteorological effects. I assume that the constant and rhythmical repetitions of the same irre-
gularities of sunshine produce in the aggregate
a chemical terrestrial sun-heat climate, for which
I will use the term *our* sun; for the earth and
chemistry this our sun never sets or varies. The
general quantity of heat supplied to the earth
never practically fluctuates, and is eternally constant; and it will be my task to show that just
as the mean of the varying effects of the sun
and things meteorological called climate produces results on the earth's fauna and vegetation,
so the analogous mean of sun-heat, which I will
call our sun, or the chemical sun-heat climate,
produces also decided actions on the earth's
minerals, that is, on chemistry. The quantity'

of heat receivable from a heat source is inversely
as the square of the distance, hence the always
limited amount of matter that the near heat source,
fire, may heat, receives from it more heat than
that same matter does from *our* sun ; hence one
reason that fire's action, for limited quantities of
matter, is more powerful and violent than that of
our sun on the same matter: this is one important
difference in the action of sun and fire heats.
Again, fire effects are completely partial, and not
constantly rhythmically repeated, as the sun's are,
and thus we can easily detect fire effects on the
background of contrast of the many things not
acted on by fire : we can compare things that were
in a fire with things that were never near fire; we
can take a fire away or it itself dies out.   But our
sun's effects are universal and continuously unceasing, and everything on earth, we ourselves, have
been, and are always, in *our* sun's fire, and have
as much as we can take of its heat, and this, our
sun, we cannot take away or put out ; hence, for
this sun-heat of things we have not a vestige of
a background of contrast or of comparison, and
the curious but natural result arises, that of many
of the effects of our sun-heat, especially of those
that are analogues of the well-known fire *latent*
heat, we are utterly physically and mentally un-
conscious, as we are of the pressure of the atmos-

phere. Whoever thinks of or ·feels the sun-got
latent heat in chemicals or in himself? Nevertheless all things and beings have, some a great deal,
and all as much of the heat of *our* sun latent in
them as their varying capacities for heat will allow
them to take; and this for the simple but cogent
reason that there is such an endowment in chemicals and beings as heat capacity, and since our
sun does undeniably heat the earth, and chemicals,
and all things. Sun-got latent heat, therefore,
necessarily exists, although its universality makes
it latent or hidden indeed, and so undemonstrable
by the means that at once indicate fire-got latent
heat—the means, namely, of contrast with fire-
unaffected objects; and further, the sun-got latent
heat's universality makes it also imperceptible to
our physical senses. For it is a law in our nature
that we do not readily perceive effects that are
continuous and unceasing, and which we and all
things participate, and for which therefore there is
no ready means of comparison. An antediluvian
child marked easily the crawling course of a snail
against the near background of contrast, such as a
still leaf; well, to perceive the vastly swifter earth
motions, for which there is no nearer background
of contrast than heavenly bodies, it took, after the
lapse of ages, not a few ripe minds: it is therefore not altogether unnatural that we should think,

write, and experiment much on fire-got latent heat,
and little or nothing on the very unobtrusive but
really theoretically and generally far more important sun latent heat. I repeat, for all chemicals, and for the entire globe, which we are going
to regard as but a greater chemical, having properties the average of those of all its component
chemicals, there exists a great unique heat source,
namely, our sun; it never sets, nor varies, nor
dies out. In chemicals, and also in the greatest
chemical, the earth in totality, there exists the endowment called specific heat, and others of which
we are soon to treat. Can it be possible that
this sun fire, nature's sole and great heat agent,
has had no effect on chemicals so aptly constituted
for heat effects? Can sun-heat have had effects
that are trivial and unimportant? is what we should
rather ask ourselves. The problem, therefore, we
have to place before our minds is not so much the
proof of the existence of latent sun-heat effects on
chemicals—they cannot be logically denied—but
the nature of these effects. The effects of sun-
heat and fire-heat, since the two are identical
forces, are the same, apart from the important
modifications produced by the presence of the entire earth, by the universality and distance of the
sun and the nearness and partiality of fire. For
all fire-heat's effects we have therefore modified

analogues in our sun-heat; and this is so far a
great help, for we have only to ascertain what fire
effects are, and then to deduct from them, as it
were, certain modifications, and we shall have the
sun-heat effects themselves. It becomes therefore
a *sine quâ non* that we should first thoroughly
grasp the effects of fire on matter, and no pains-
taking must be grudged, if necessary, to master
these dry details, for without them it is vain
to think of comprehending the phenomena of
chemical action, or the more recondite effects of
sun-heat on matter.

CHAPTER II.

Fire effects on matter : thermometric and latent heat : heat conduction. Heat becomes latent in dilating matter, in bringing matter nearer to fusion or vaporisation, in fusing and vaporising matter : several kinds of latent heats all producing more or less dilatation ; their names and the capacities for them. Constant correlation of heat to dilatation, &c., of matter.

FIRE heats matter and transforms it. Fire heats or affects matter in two ways: it gives matter thermometric heat, and it gives matter heat latent. And the transformations that fire impresses upon matter are also two : first, simple dilatation; second, dilatation with the two fluidities. Hence heat has a very important, invariable, inseparable correlation with matter's dilatation and transformation. Such is a very broad statement of the general effects on making fire-heat. But we must study these fire effects much more in detail. Let us put equal weights of carbon and silver, at the same distances, before a fire; if we then examine the silver, we find that before the fire it becomes thermometrically hot sooner than the carbon, and will always feel hotter to us before a fire, and will also feel colder to us than carbon if the two be on a very cold object; for silver not only readily

takes heat, but as readily gives it; and this property of silver is called conduction of heat, and
the power of heat conduction is termed conductivity. Conductivity is therefore a dualistic property: it is the property of giving and taking
thermometric heat; it is alike affected by a source
of heat and a source, so to speak, of cold; from
the former it takes heat, and to the latter it, in
like ratio, gives. Carbon conducts heat worse
than silver, that is, takes more time to receive
thermometric heat or to give it away; and so
slowly do some chemicals give and take thermometric heat that they are called non-conductors.
But after a time carbon and silver, before the fire,
get equally thermometrically hot, and if the two
then touch, they can neither give nor take their
fire-got heat from each other; and yet the silver
and carbon before the fire never get really equally
hot; though the thermometer seems at first to say
so, they never have equal quantity of heat in
them, allowing me for the present such expres-
sions; for if silver and carbon be taken from the
fire, and each placed in a vessel of an ounce of
water at 0°, and there left to cool, then the water in
carbon's vessel is found by the thermometer itself
hotter than that in silver's vessel: therefore it
used to be argued that carbon can hold more heat,
has greater heat capacity than silver. The excess

of heat that carbon held over silver we find, therefore, that a thermometer does not indicate, since
the thermometer pronounced the two equally hot.
It is therefore a heat latent, and to distinguish it
from other heat latents, we will call it specifically
latent heat; and the power that carbon or chemicals have of making heat thus latent in them,
we will call the specific latent-heat capacity. It
is a very important power in chemicals, and has
been found to be inversely as their equivalents;
and this capacity is also a double one, for if carbon has the power of, so to speak, filling itself
with heat near a fire, carbon has also the power
of emptying itself of heat to a like amount in the
cold water where carbon was put. It must be
further observed that the heat that carbon made
by its specific heat capacity, latent in itself, carbon took from the fire and gave out again to the
water as thermometric heat, and thus it was only
when retained in the carbon that the heat assumed
the latent phase. Let us now again place the
carbon and silver, and an equal weight of ice, at
equal distances, before a fire, and we shall find
that the fire not only heats all three, but affects
their forms also. The carbon, fire simply dilates,
and nothing else. The silver, fire dilates, but it
also approaches silver to its melting point, which
we cannot strictly say of carbon, for no fire fuses

carbon; or the fire may completely melt silver.
The ice, fire irregularly dilates, and will readily
transform into fluid water, or even expand into
gaseous steam. And if we observe all these heat-
given changes in form, we find more or less of
expansion in them; hence the transformations of
matter by fire-heat is either one of simple expansion or it may be one of expansion plus a fluidity,
which last is very generally only a greater expansion than the simple one. The form of simple
expansion fire in the long-run always gives to
matter; the expansion with one or two fluidities
fire very generally does. Let us return again to
carbon that is before a fire, and there we find it
expanded, that is, specifically lighter; and this
expansion is undoubtedly the effect of heat, but of
this heat also that expands carbon the thermometer gives no accurate indication, it is therefore
also heat latent, and dilatation itself has also its
latent heat, which shall be termed expansively
latent heat, and the power of carbon and chemicals
of rendering heat expansively latent in them I will
call expansive latent-heat capacity. If we regard
silver before the fire, we find that it has also
dilated and approached to melting, if not actually
melted. And in this approach to fusion, heat becomes also latent; for we know that capacity for
heat increases with heating, and silver at 200°, or

140° nearer melting, holds more latent heat (allow the expression) than silver at 60°. Here therefore is a third latent heat that is connected with fusion and boiling points, which we shall call the preparatory latent heat, since it seems occupied in preparing matter for a change of state, and the power of making heat so latent I will term the preparatory latent-heat capacity. If we now regard ice before a fire, we find that it also has expanded very greatly, and passed into steam; and in steam we know, since the time of Dr Black, that there is a great deal of latent heat. This latent heat I will term Black's or fluidly latent heat, and the power of rendering heat so latent I will call the fluid latent-heat capacity. It is important, therefore, for our future guidance and reasoning, to acknowledge and grant the existence of these four kinds of latent heats—namely, the fluidly, the preparatory, the specifically, the expansively latent heats—and the four corresponding capacities in matter for them. All these four latent heats—first, second, third, and fourth—are producing the same kind of action, namely, expansion, which, however, differs in degree and value in the order of the numerals I have attached to them. Further, all these degrees of latent heat invariably give each its correlated property to matter. If we see steam or any gas, we know that in it and them must exist fluidly latent heat.   Silver 2° from fusion has more preparatory latent heat than silver at natural states.   A specifically lighter carbon has more expansively latent heat in it than a heavier carbon, and so on.   By bringing several chemicals before a fire, therefore, we have learned something; we shall also learn somewhat by taking them away.

CHAPTER III.

Of the entire globe as but a great chemical: the earth has a heat
constitution of her own; that is, latent heats, with capacities
for them, mass, and conductivity: the earth as a whole thus
acts on single chemicals in a manner antagonistic to the sun
force: thence we can deduce the true nature of latent heat.
The two great balancing forces in chemistry: the positive and
negative, our sun and our earth: the meaning of the terms:
the general mode of action on chemicals of our sun and earth:
this action in detail upon gold, platinum, oxygen, nitrogen,
carbon, sulphur. Causes of the forms of the elements. Origin
of the heat of combustion: of the latent heats of natural and
permanent gases: reason of their permanency. Why the gas
steam burns us and the gas oxygen does not. The action of
our sun and earth on other elements, as metals, chlorine, the
other halogens, phosphorus. The nature of allotropies.

WHEN we take chemicals heated and transformed
by a fire away from it, they, as a rule, gradually
cool and retransform into their pristine shapes.
Why? Because, according to the views to be
advocated in this work, the fire-heated chemicals,
when fire is taken away, forsake the partial,
temporary heat-equilibrium of fire, which they,
by virtue of the heat capacities and properties
just considered, had taken, and reassume, by virtue
of the identical heat endowments, the general
everlasting heat-equilibrium of all things around
them, which our sun has long ago struck with the

globe. But latent heats are all correlated to
form or states and certain physical properties of
chemicals; and in taking our sun's general,
instead of fire's partial, equilibrium, the chemicals
resume with their old latent heats their old forms
and properties. The fire-heated chemicals are surrounded by a vast mass of matter; our earth,
which is but a greater chemical, the mean of her
chemicals, she cools them when the fire is taken
away down to her own heat level, by virtue of the
great forces of her own heat constitution, which
corresponds exactly to that of her chemicals, only
in the last the forces of the heat constitution are
in miniature, and in the earth, as a whole, they
are gigantic and perfect. These forces are the
earth's four degrees of latent heat, known approximatively by her specific gravity, her general
form, her fusibility and volatility, &c., the earth's
capacity for each of these latent heats and her
conductivity; the totality of all of which I will
term earth force. The effect of this earth force
is necessarily more or less on every chemical, and
is balanced by our sun's force. At present, when
a chemist thinks or theorises about a chemical,
say ice or water, he does so as if he and the ice
or water existed as absolutely isolated things in
nature. This is surely scientifically false. The
ice belongs chemically to the earth, and the ice

and the earth are bound thermally and chemically
to our sun. Two enormous chemical forces are
indissolubly linked in the apparently isolated bit
of ice a chemist may hold in his hand, our sun's
heat and the earth force. The forces of the earth's
heat constitution appeal to the precisely similar
forces in miniature in the ice, and without
ceasing urge them strongly to a mutual equilibrium. And if no other force step in to help the
ice, it will always obey the earth's forces and
remain ice; but if sun force or heat appear and
preponderate, ice takes the heat, and will melt
into water or pass into vapour—that is, ice, by
its heat constitution or endowments, will take an
equilibrium in which sun-heat or force preponderates, and as latent heat is correlated to form
and expansively changes it, ice will then be expanded into vapour. But in water vapour there
is still the four degrees of latent heat, and the
capacities for them, and a certain conductivity—
that is, there is still in vapour the endowments
that link it and all chemicals to the greater
chemical, the globe; there is, therefore, still earth
force acting on vapour, and trying to bring it
down to earth-force equilibrium or level. So
that sun-heat, to produce water vapour from ice
at all, must coerce the earth force, or rather
balance it. The sun-heat, therefore, in water

vapour is a force fully occupied in mastering the
earth force. Hence this sun-heat is latent, hidden from the mercury of thermometers; for it
cannot dilate that mercury the smallest fraction
of a degree, for the sun-heat is fully occupied in
analogously dilating the ice into vapour against
the earth force. To hold mercury, the force must,
as it were, let go the water vapour, and this happens when the vapour again becomes ice; for ice
is more at equilibrium with the earth force. Ice
has a latent heat more in correspondence with
the general latent heat of the globe, and ice has
also a correlated solid form more akin to that
which our earth generally affects. Hence ice is not
in such a position of constraint to the earth force
as vapour is, and little extraneous force is necessary
to keep water here on earth as ice, and the earth-
force constraining power, sun-heat, that existed in
water vapour is disoccupied when that vapour becomes ice, and we can utilise this force since it is
disoccupied in dilating thermometric mercury, or in
giving us through our nerves to our sensorium the
feeling of heat. The just chemical idea of sun-
heat latent in water vapour, therefore, is not that
it is there latent or hidden, for we find that sun-
heat in vapour is doing the very hard work of
coercing the great earth's force. Nor, indeed, is
the term potential, as a name for this latent heat,

so well suited to chemistry as physics, for chemistry is a science in which transformations play
a leading part. Hence we might, in our chemical theory (were it not for the inconvenience of
changing even inappropriate names), call this
heat latent in water vapour, and indeed all latent
heats, morphigenic heat—that is, heat occupied
in the production of form; heat taken up in
shaping, moulding earth's matter; and as earth
matter, reduced to a typical generality, is solid,
this said morphigenic heat is occupied in giving
more or less dilated forms to solidities; and thermometric heat will be heat disoccupied, available,
amorphigenic.

So that there exist in nature two great chemical
forces, our sun and our earth, and we must in
chemistry take the two always conjointly together,
or we shall seldom understand the action of either.
By our sun is meant the sun-heat climate of the
globe, which climate, though it be the aggregate
result of hourly, daily, monthly, yearly varying
sun-effects, yet it itself never varies, and the long-
run average supply of sun-heat to our globe is
a fixed quantity. This fixed quantity is our sun.
That a certain result occurs from ceaseless repetitions of uncertainties, we make out from the
calculations of life insurance. Nothing, surely,
can be more variable than the duration of a single

human life, or indeed of a hundred human lives.
But when we get, say a million repetitions of
such lives, an average life may be struck from
them, and assumed of such accuracy of constancy
that we may daily, practically, and safely act upon
it. As this typical, unvarying insurance life is to
common lives, so is our sun's heat to the constantly varying effects of usual sun-heat. But to
the term *our earth* we also attach a special meaning. Our earth is one vast average chemical, composed of all her many chemicals, and having all the
heat properties in average of all her chemicals.
Our earth will have, therefore, in average, her own
degrees of latent heat and latent-heat capacities
and conductivity; and these heat properties, small
in her comparatively minute chemicals, become
colossal in the earth as a vast whole. Our earth's
amount of expansively latent heat is deducible
approximatively from her mass: her specifically,
preparatory, and fluidly latent heats may be
gathered from the fusibility and volatility of the
general matter of the earth; and the capacities
for these latent heats may in a measure be arrived
at from the very form the earth has finally taken
under the sun's action; and the earth's conductivity, we shall find, may be ascertained from
telegraphy. So that a sufficiently precise idea can
be formed of the earth, as but a large chemical,

to render her valuable in chemical theoretical
research and reasoning. We assert, therefore, that
our sun and this so heat-constituted earth are
great chemical forces, and must act and react
constantly, powerfully, on every chemical by means
of the similar heat constitution in chemicals, their
mass, latent-heat capacities and conductivities.
These properties in chemicals are not merely
curious laboratory endowments, but are active in
nature, and are dualistic, or have a double function,
and exist alike for the coldness that our earth
represents, as for heat which our sun personifies.
Our sun and our earth are therefore antagonistic
forces. The one force, our sun, even thus early
may be seen to be the positive force of nature;
and the other force, our earth, to be the negative.
Our sun tries to impress on a chemical his positive
form of matter, involving more or less the presence
of latent heat and some of the correlated dilatation;
our earth endeavours to produce in the same chemical the negative or earth form of matter, one involving more or less diminution of latent heat with
some degree of correlated contraction. For we
know that heat gives dilated forms to matter, and
matter left entirely to the earth, the sun being
taken away, solidifies. But in nature neither our
sun nor our earth ever get completely the better
of one another. In every chemical in the world

there is, so to speak, both sun and earth influence; what may happen, however, is, that one of the two forces may in a chemical preponderate over the other; for the heat constitution of chemicals differs widely. Some have constitutions more suitable for our earth to work on, and others have heat endowments more fitted for our sun's influence; and lastly, there are chemicals greatly sensitive to the actions of the two forces, such as we have seen water to be. The properties that will on this globe make sun effects to preponderate in a chemical are, as a rule, small mass, great heat capacity, and non-conductivity. The properties that will make our earth preponderate in a chemical are, as a rule, great mass, small heat capacities, good conductivity. The endowments that will render a chemical sensitive to the action of both forces are usually high heat capacity, average mass, and not good conductivity. In order to study in detail the effects of these, our two great chemical forces on chemicals, let us first take elements, and of these such as are extensively present, free in nature, for such are most likely to have sprung from general or all-reaching causes; we take, therefore, oxygen, nitrogen, carbon, sulphur, and gold and platinum. All these occur extensively free in nature; with the production of none, except perhaps sulphur, a

partial, local cause seems to have been at work.
Of these elements we also choose for study the
ultimate particles, with a view of early impressing
on the mind that our two forces act on ultimate
particles as well as on the largest masses, and also
to facilitate our future conception of the correlation of latent heat to certain motions of earth
matter. Of the particles of the elements above
mentioned, the golden and platinal ones will be
greatly affected by our earth, and not so much by
our sun ; for platinum and gold are massive, and
have large equivalents (about 98 and 99); and as
heat capacity is inversely as the equivalent, and
is still more diminished by amount of mass, gold
and platinum have small heat capacities and good
conductivity. So that the heat our sun gives gold
and platinum has, first of all, much matter in them
to heat, and that matter is so constituted as to be
more ready, by its conductivity, to give heat away
thermometrically than to make morphigenic use
of it by making it latent ; and in connection with
the platinal and golden matter is our vast, latently
cold earth, as willing to take heat as gold and platinum to give. Hence in gold and platinum we see
little of that expansion, with the correlated latent
heat, that our sun tends to give to matter. They
are heavy and not very fusible, and want greatly
all the degrees of latent heat—namely, the ex-

pansive, preparatory, or fluidly latent heats. They
are what I shall in future term latently cold or
negative or earthlike elements. In nature gold
and platinum are before two forces, our sun and
earth, representing heat and cold, positive and
negative. Gold and platinum, from their heat
constitution, must take from our sun thermometric
and latent heat, but by the double function of the
same heat constitution, they must give both heats
to our latently cold earth in like measure. The
thermometric heat that gold receives from our sun
passes through gold as such, and is given out as
such by virtue of gold's conductivity alone. The
latent heat in gold passes in and out as thermometric heat, but is detained as latent; so that in the
changes of latent heat, or in its passage through
gold, not only gold's conductivity is concerned, but
gold's capacity for heat also; so that in order to
take in or give out, or change latent heat well,
gold must possess not one heat property but two
—namely, good conductivity and heat capacity.
The latter gold has not, and its latent heat never
leaves it so much as that of some other elements,
as carbon. Gold is not utterly infusible, and also
never rises in its compounds to high states of
latent heat.

Nitrogen and oxygen have small mass and
great capacity for heat, or power of rendering heat

latent in them, as seen by their small equivalents
and mass, and the two have gaseous or the worst
conductivity; consequently the two have slowly
and greatly taken latent heat from our powerful
and eternal sun, and are thus the gases of the
atmosphere. But to oxygen and nitrogen exists also
our vast and much latently colder earth, which, in
virtue of the colossal forces of her heat constitution, will endeavour to cool these two very latently
hot gases of their sun-got latent heat; but this
our earth can do only as the powers of latent-heat
cooling or change that oxygen and nitrogen have
will allow her. Now the powers of latent-heat
cooling or change depend on capacity for heat and
conductivity. As latent heat must pass out earthwards from oxygen and nitrogen as thermometric
heat, our earth must take the latent heat out of
oxygen and nitrogen as thermometric heat if she
takes it at all; but then oxygen and nitrogen do
not conduct heat, hence our earth cannot cool
the sun-got latent heat present in non-conductive
oxygen and nitrogen, and they remain the permanent gases of the atmosphere. It is therefore
the non-conductivity of free, gaseous oxygen that
prevents it from rapidly latently cooling down to
our earth's latent coldness, in which act of cooling
gaseous oxygen must take some correlated contracted
or solid form; for oxygen has high heat capacity.

This oxygenic want of conductivity, however, we can virtually annul by adding a conductor or a suitable metal to oxygen ; and when a heat-capacious metal is in close contact with oxygen, we have a union of oxygen's great heat capacity with the metal's conductivity, and then very rapid cooling of oxygen's sun-got latent heat occurs, and we see oxygen, in partnership or compounded with the metal, discharge great heat into our earth, or burn, and, in the metallic oxide resulting, assume our earth's latent coldness, with a correlated solid form often surprisingly like the general matter of the earth. And why nitrogen does not so act shall hereafter be explained. But it may be objected that if free oxygen had in it the great heat before combustion with a metal that we see during that combustion, that that heat in the free oxygen would burn us, for we are constantly touching oxygen; but we are not burnt by atmospheric oxygen, because the heat in it is heat latent, obtained from our sun. We and oxygen are equally present to our sun; we both are equally near it, and welcome to take directly from it as much heat as we can take; and we both do take it, and if we do not take more, it is because neither can. How, then, can either take second-hand from the other what is not taken first-hand or directly from our sun himself? If you refuse to take the heat from our sun, you must refuse to take the same heat from oxygen. Two objects that have existed constantly, equally near to our sun, cannot exchange his latent heat with each other; and indeed we saw this distinctly happen with respect to fire-heat, that is, to silver and carbon that we placed before a fire. After a time carbon and silver before a fire, though each was very differently latently hot, yet the two when touching did not exchange any of their latent heat as long as they were before the fire. Hence one of the difficulties of demonstrating sun-got latent heat; hence oxygen and nitrogen are what is termed permanent gases, for they cannot get anything around to cool them of the heat that has made them gases, that is, sun-got latent heat, of which everything around them is as saturated as they themselves. For common physical contact, therefore, no exchange of sun-got latent heat in chemicals occurs; we shall, however, presently find that on chemical, that is, molecular, very close contact, such latent-heat exchanges happen, and constitute what is generally called chemical action. It is also different with chemicals having fire-got latent heat. Nothing in nature around has been so near the fire as the steam that thence sprung; having therefore been nearer a near heat source, fire, than all things around it, steam has more latent

heat than all things around, for they have only the
heat of the far source, our sun. Hence all things
around fire-sprung steam will take heat from it,
that is, will cool steam down to our earth and
sun-heat level or to water. We ourselves, also,
being heat-equilibrised to our sun, and not to fire,
must, however unwillingly, take heat from steam,
and get thereby burnt.

The heat, therefore, that we see during metallic
combustion is heat that has been ultimately
derived from our sun, and is latent in gaseous
oxygen, occupied in keeping that oxygen a gas
amid surrounding or preponderating earth solidity.
It is sun force in gaseous oxygen there constraining
earth forces, and therefore latent; and as during
metallic oxidation or combustion gaseous oxygen
solidifies, it then loses the position of constraint
to our solid earth, and disoccupies the constraining
sun force or heat that was in gaseous oxygen, and
the heat consequently appears in the thermometric
phase, and will burn us. Of the combustion of
carbon we shall treat further on.

Carbon has both conductivity, small mass, and
good heat capacity; hence carbon enjoys excellent
powers of taking heat in all its phases, and also
of giving it away; hence carbon is one of the
most important of the elements, and one of the
heat links of all phases between our sun and earth;

and with the last two carbon exchanges perfectly
both thermometric and latent heat. But latent
heat is correlated to form (as shall be even better
seen hereafter); hence with this great power of
latent-heat exchanges of carbon, known by its
small mass and small equivalent and good conductivity, there must exist also as great a correlated power of form exchange or of transformations; and we thus get our first glimpse of the
peculiar fitness of carbon for the essential place
it occupies in organic chemistry, the transformations of which are marvellously extensive.

Carbon in nature, however, as long as it is in
contact only with our earth, will give her, in virtue
of its constitution, its heat of all phases, and will
become perfectly and in all respects latently earth
cold or negative, far more than gold; for one of
the requisites of latent-heat cooling, capacity for
heat, is far greater in carbon than in gold. We
find, therefore, free carbon the most latently cold
or negative element known, the most infusible,.
the most solid; for so far is free carbon from
liquidity, that it never singly or uncompounded
reaches it; for present to carbon in its single or
free state is the colossal earth force, and the heat
that our sun is enabled to give carbon by virtue
of carbon's heat constitution, our vast earth by,
takes from carbon in virtue of that very same

carbonic heat constitution. Our sun, therefore,
cannot latently heat free carbon; and even the
larger amount of heat that fire can give to single
carbon, our vast earth by, takes and neutralises:
so intimate are the heat connections of our earth
and carbon, upon which, indeed, depends the very
existence of the organic kingdom. But if something beside our vast latently cold earth be present to carbon, and be in molecular contact with
it—and that something be, unlike our earth,
latently hot or positive, as is highly gaseous
oxygen—then the very same heat attributes of
carbon, small mass, great heat capacity, and good
conductivity, that made carbon take the infusible
earth or latent coldness, will now make carbon
touching the latently hot gaseous oxygen take
oxygen's shape or latent heat, that is, will make
carbon gaseous, as we know happens when oxygen, as is said, combines with carbon, producing
carbonic anhydrid gas. That carbon, therefore, if
free or single, with our latently cold earth by,
cannot be fused, is no proof that carbon is intrinsically infusible. We actually see many instances
in which carbon is liquid or gaseous, as an ingredient of its organic and inorganic compounds.
In such combinations carbon has been even easily
gasified or liquefied, and precisely for the same
reasons and heat constitution that made carbon

single, with our earth by, impossible to liquefy.
We find that carbon is well fitted to take sun
forms, or to become latently hot or unliquefiably
gaseous; and the reason is, that carbon has high
heat capacity, its equivalent being 6, and small
mass and conductivity. But with such a heat
constitution we yet find free carbon here on earth,
having the most earth form, being the most
latently cold or negative element, the most solid
that is infusible of those elements; and it must
be so, for the heat constitution of chemicals has a
dualistic function; and what it is to heat, it is
also impartially to cold. Now to free carbon is
alone present always our vast, latently cold earth;
and carbon is indeed never single, for our earth
always looms by, and our earth's latent coldness
or negativeness reacts in free carbon and cools it,
and keeps it cooled to her level, provided our
earth gets carbon all to herself, as she does when
carbon is thought to be single and free. If it be
free or single, our earth can coerce carbon's heat
states; and free carbon in nature might by a
mechanical mind be likened to a strong spring
bent down and so held by our earth, just as
oxygen might be thought a spring bent up and
kept *in situ* by our sun. But our latently cold
earth does not get carbon always entirely to herself. Sometimes oxygen, that we have found is

full (allow the expression) of sun-got latent heat,
comes between our earth and carbon—comes by
reason of certain attraction, soon to be considered,
into the closest molecular contact with carbon,
and then comes a struggle for the possession of
carbon between the latent heat that is in oxygen,
and the latent coldness or negativeness that is in
our vast earth. And we know that the latent heat
that is in oxygen gains the day. Carbon combines
with oxygen, leaves its solid shape for a gaseous
one, forming carbonic anhydrid gas, and this
greatly because of carbon's own heat constitution;
and further, because of the intense nearness of
the oxygen to carbon and our earth's comparative distance; this because also of the excellent
heat capacity of oxygen itself: and thus carbon
with oxygen leaps up into carbonic anhydrid gas,
earth loosened into the highest sun forms, approach-
ing that of oxygen itself, for the heat capacities
of carbon are near those of oxygen: but the oxy-
terric struggle for carbon is arduous; our earth
has greatly in her favour her immensity, but then
she is far off, and her forces decrease with distance;
but even so, for freeing carbon from our earth's
control, oxygen requires always, as we know, the
further assistance of heat on carbon: we always,
for oxycarbonic combination, have to set fire to
carbon.

Sulphur has mass greater and heat capacity inferior to those of oxygen and nitrogen, and also greater conductivity, so sulphur has not the high latent-heat forms of nitrogen and oxygen. Again, sulphur has not the conductivity of gold, platinum, or carbon; hence though sulphur is a solid, its style of solidity is very different from that of platinum, gold, and carbon. Sulphur's solidity is a light one, and is one also that is near gaseity, sulphur being volatile. The golden, platinal, and carbonic solidities are heavier, and much further from liquidity and gaseity than sulphur's. Sulphur, therefore, though a solid, yet is a solid near gaseity, and thus of a latently hot or positive description. Sulphur's solidity differs from the most predominant solidity of nature, which is that of our earth's, a rather heavy and infusible solidity; in sulphur, therefore, there is still a constraining force needful to retain in sulphur its positive volatile solidity, and this constraining force is derived from our sun, and is sulphur's sun-got latent heat. The solidities we find in chemistry are very unlike each other. For example, the solids of the anhydrids of acids are very different from those of the bases. The anhydrid solid is fusible, soluble, volatile, light, often unstable; the basic solid is often of the greatest stability, heavier, much less fusible—often not at all so, not

so soluble or volatile, and the forms of the two
solids, correlated to their latent heats, differ also
as greatly; the anhydrid solid is unlike, in aspect
and nature, the general type of the solids of the
earth, whereas the basic solid is so like the prevailing earth-solidity as to be often called *par
excellence* " earths." The anhydrids, in fact, we
shall hereafter find, are types of the latently hot
or positive compound solids, and the bases of the
latently cold or negative ones. Passing now to
the examination of the elements generally, we find
many metals capable of existing free in nature,
that is, between our sun and earth forces, because
such metals' heat constitution are more favourable
for terrestrial influences; but many of even these
metals are not strictly or perfectly permanent, for
reason better divined in potassium's greater
changeableness. Potassium is light, fusible, volatile, and has, therefore, a good deal of the solar
or positive, or latently hot form, and is thus not
at equilibrium with our earth's form or latent heat;
but potassium is also light, heat capacious, and
conductive, and has thus some power of taking
earth-equilibrium, or discharging latent heat. And
further, potassium meets around metalloids as
oxygen, that more than it lack and seek earth-
equilibrium, and to which potassium can supply
conductivity; hence potassium never occurs free,

c

but always combined or earth-equilibrised with
some metalloid, and having, when thus compounded, a resemblance to "earths." To keep
potassium free is a difficult task; even under
naphtha, the earth and sun forces react on potassium, and cover it with an allotropic crust; for
free potassium is not a child of nature or of our
sun, but of furnace heat, and its equilibrium taken
with furnace heat must become slowly changed to
that of our sun. There exist two metals, hydrogen
and mercury, that have, the first, the highest, and
the second a high latent-heat form; for hydrogen
is an unliquified gas, and quicksilver a fluid. But
hydrogen, though it conducts heat the best of all
gases, and has thus a highly important amount of
heat conduction, cannot be said to have a maximum metallic conductivity; and having least mass
and equivalent, and hence the best-known heat
capacity, does reach permanently, even single, the
highest of latent-heat or solar form. Mercury has
also, for a metal, bad conductivity, and having
large equivalent and weight, and small heat capacity, lacks greatly both the necessaries of rapid
latent-heat cooling; so that although mercury may
take heat from unnaturally strong heat-forces, as
the common or volcanic fire, still, having only a
natural cooling source—our earth—does not so
readily latently cool down to her level, and remains

fluid; and of all fluids mercury presents a coherence
most like that of solidity, and runs in globules.
Nothing can be more different than the liquids met
with in chemistry; and they too may be divided
into a positive latently hot class, or a negative or
latently cold class, according to their relations
to mass and gaseity or to mass and solidity—their
relation to sun or earth forms or latent heat. At
the foot, or negative end of the latent-heat scale
for liquids, stands quicksilver, chiefly through its
great weight, which deteriorates its heat capacity,
and impedes thus its chemical activity. At the
top, or positive end of the latent-heat scale for
liquids, stands such fluids as the ethers and
alcohol by their lightness, and great, even un-
known distance, from solidification and their great
volatility. Among solids, as we have seen, there
exists also the negative and the positive types:
the positive metals are light, heat capacious, fusible, and it may be even volatile, as potassium, &c.;
the negative metals are heavier, less heat capacious, with tendency to infusibility, as platinum, &c.;
and this division of metals becomes necessary for
the study of galvanism. When we examine chlorine, bromine, and iodine, we remark distinctly
enough the influence of mass, heat capacity, and
conductivity on elemental latent heat and its
correlated form. Of the three halogens, chlorine

has the most gaseous positive latently hot form,
for chlorine has of the three the smallest mass
and equivalent, and thus the best heat capacity,
and a gaseous or worst conductivity. Bromine
has a form or latent heat less positive or solar
than chlorine, being liquid, and bromine has more
mass and equivalent, and worse heat capacity
and more conductivity, than chlorine. Finally,
iodine, being solid, has a form less solar or positive
than gaseous chlorine or liquid bromine, and
iodine has most mass and equivalent and conductivity, and least heat capacity. These three
halogens seldom, if ever, occur free in nature;
their comparative nearness to earth-equilibrium,
the existence of metals to aid them in reaching
equilibrium by annulling their non-conductivity,
renders the attainment of earth-equilibrium by
these elements, by metallic combination, so easy
that it is sure to take place. In chlorine we also
observe an elemental gas more latently cold or negative than oxygen and nitrogen. For just as there
are in chemistry great differences among the latent-
heat states of its solidities and liquidities, so also
there are dissimilarities among its gaseities. Some
gases there are that are heavy and near their
liquefaction, and such are more latently cold or
negative than such gases as are light and far from
liquefaction. Hence, at the top of the gaseous

latent-heat scale must be placed, as the most
latently hot or positive body known, light and
unliquefiable hydrogen, and in the gas chlorine we
have already reached a considerable latent gaseous
negativeness, for chlorine gas is much heavier and
more liquefiable than is hydrogen. If we consider
iodine, we find that its capacity for heat, as seen
merely by its equivalent (125), seemingly smaller
than that of gold (99), and yet iodine has a
much higher latent-heat form than gold ; but the
real intrinsic heat capacity of a chemical is influenced by its mass as well as by its equivalent.
If a chemical has mass as 1, and another chemical mass as 2, and both the same equivalent,
the chemical with the mass as 1 will have really
the greater heat capacity, since having half the
matter it can yet hold the same amount of heat.
Hence, if we multiply gold's and iodine's equivalents by their weights, we find the result for
iodine 617, and for gold 1910·7 ; and these numbers might be taken as indicating more truly their
heat capacities.

In phosphorus we find considerable mass, and
not very small equivalent, and conductivity better
than sulphur's ; and phosphorus has therefore not
very high heat capacity, and yet common waxy
phosphorus has a high latent-heat form, because
its heat equilibrium is not taken with our sun

and earth, but with furnace heat. When waxy
phosphorus is put into water, the forces of our sun
and earth act upon it, and the white allotropy of
phosphorus is assumed, and this form of phosphorus is latently colder than the waxy form,
being heavier and more infusible. But in even
this white latently colder variety of phosphorus
too much of the furnace heat still remains latent,
and if you heat this or common phosphorus in
inactive gases to melting, and keep it for some
time so heated, then in this state the phosphoric
particles, having the fluid facility of motion, and
also the fluid increase of heat capacity, are able to
effect the necessary latent-heat changes, and to
take a perfect terro-solar latent-heat equilibrium,
by becoming latently colder, heavier, more infusible, as the red allotropy of phosphorus.
Hence the allotropies of phosphorus and other
chemicals are traceable to their heat endowments,
and to the pressure put upon them by the great
chemical forces of fire, that is, of a sun in miniature and nearer than natural, or of our sun and
of our earth. Allotropies are therefore of the same
nature as any of the other form changes that latent
heat gives to matter, and allotropic effects are
correlated to latent heat as the other more familiar
heat effects of dilatation, &c., are : hence we have
a fifth kind of latent heat in chemistry, the allo-

tropic, intimately connected with the other degrees
of latent heat and with the surprising transformations of allotropy; and·of this heat latent we
shall hereafter treat when on the subject of chemical transformations.

CHAPTER IV.

No isolation for any chemical in nature ; our sun and earth's influence reach all : and this often explains the violence of some
chemical actions.   Our sun's heat acting on the heat capacity
of chemicals, that differs in all chemicals, produces in them
differences or disequilibria of their latent heats.   The signs of
this latent-heat difference or disequilibria.   The disequilibrium
not felt in the usual contact of matter, but greatly felt by
chemicals on their molecular or chemical contact.   The various
latent-heat disequilibria between chemicals.   There is a constant effort at rectifying these latent-heat disequilibria by
chemical action, which consists in heat discharges leading to
latent-heat equilibrium of the actors.   Between chemical combining actors, latent-heat disequilibrium at the beginning of
their action, and equilibrium at its close, are always demonstrable.

WE find, therefore, that chemicals on earth, existing as they all do before our sun-fire, have there
behaved pretty much as they do before a common
fire ; except that our sun cannot act with partiality,
and if our sun necessarily affects the minutest
particle in the world, he also as unavoidably
reacts on the largest masses, even to our earth
herself.   Again, though chemical particles are
thus before the sun-fire and subject to sun-force,
yet, being on the world, they are part of the whole,
and are there surrounded by a great mass of

matter, and are thus subject to that also, or to
our earth's power. There is no such thing as isolation in chemistry even for the tiniest atom; all
particles, all chemicals in nature, are linked by
certain forces into inextricable, viewless union—
into one vast whole. Yet when we see two molecules in violent chemical action, we wonder, for
they seem so small, so weak, so isolated, because,
so thinking, we overlook the fact that it is not
the two molecules that are alone working, but
often much more, the magnificently grand and
potent forces of our sun and earth in them. When
we consider that the power that creates steam out
of water has, in doing so, coerced the herculean
earth-force, shall we be amazed to see it drive easily
the weightiest human machinery or the swiftest
train? When we think of the real and immense
forces often at play during chemical action, shall
we be startled at its intenseness and violence?
For our sun and earth undoubtedly exist, and conductivity and latent-heat capacities in chemicals
are not mere scientific or philosophically interesting curiosities, but are living and greatly active
forces in nature. The chemical elements, having
each its special capacity for heat and other heat
endowments, and being all before our everlasting
sun, have there got each very unequally sun
latently hot: nothing in chemical science is to

me truer than this, or more important. Most
matter, left to the preponderating influence of the
earth, solidifies. We can by care, &c., partially,
temporarily keep away the sun or his representative, heat, from a small portion of earth's matter—
that is, we can for a time cool bits of matter—and
when so treated, even though it be a rarefied gas,
and even though our means of producing cold are
very limited, matter often solidifies. If we had
means, therefore, of altogether taking our sun
away from our earth, and of thus producing great
cold, few will deny that all gases on earth would
solidify, and the solids would become more and
more difficult to fuse. All chemicals on earth,
therefore, that have forms or states more approach-
ing liquidity and gascity than this solid form
which our earth, if she had her own way, would
give them, have acquired those forms from a force
extraneous to our earth; and no other such force
exists except our sun, or his miniature representative, fire. That water exists in the world as cloud-
vapour, every one perceives water owes to the
sun and to water's own heat constitution. The
same is, however, also true of oxygen's gascity ;
for though oxygen through its heat constitution
exists now that the sun is present as a gas, yet,
were the sun taken away, oxygen by the same
constitution would earth-equilibrise or solidify.

The only difference is, that water's heat constitution renders it more amenable to our earth and sun's action than oxygen; but oxygen, nevertheless, is sensitive to heat actions, and in its compounds undergoes great variations in latent-heat states.

There is, therefore, undeniably sun-got latent heat in chemistry, where it plays a universal and most important part; and as each chemical element differs from another in heat constitution, every chemical element differs also in its amount of latent heat got generally, either directly from our sun, as in oxygen, nitrogen; or indirectly from chemical action with brother chemicals holding this heat, as is the case with hydrogen, chlorine, &c. The elements that are light, unliquefied gases have sun-got latent heat in greatest quantity. The elements that are liquefiable, heavier gases, come next in the latent-heat scale, in the proportions of their weight and liquefiability; then the light, volatile, unsolidifiable liquids, as ethers and alcohol; then the heavier liquids, as bromine, water, and finally, heavy and coherent mercury; then the light fusible solids, as potassium; then those that are more infusible and heavy, as platinum; and then the infusible solid carbon, the latently coldest of all the elements. From this point of view all the chemical elements are at molecular latent-heat disequilibrium with each other, some even intensely so; and not a few elements are at latent-heat disequilibrium with our earth, and free carbon with our sun. The inter-elementary or inter-chemical latent-heat disequilibrium is a molecular one, and is not urgently felt for the common contacts in nature; for in physical contact, chemicals touch partially, imperfectly, at certain limited points of their surfaces, and most of their molecules thus remain distant from each other. And for such contact, chemicals have what is tantamount to a latent-heat balance or equilibrium, but with this physical contact we have little to do in chemistry : there it is chemical contact that must alone pre-occupy us. Chemical contact is brought about by chemical attraction, and draws the ultimate molecules of one chemical close against those of another chemical throughout the entire mass, molecule against molecule; and during this extremely close molecular contact, the latent-heat differences of the touching molecules are severely felt, and lead to equilibrising latent-heat changes in the molecules taking place according to their heat constitutions; and then we see often heat phenomena going on, and *chemical combining action* is said to occur.

Chemical combining action, therefore, consists of attraction, molecular contact, producing heat discharges, ending in latent-heat equilibrium, with the correlated transformations between given chemicals.

Latent-heat disequilibrium is, therefore, the primary cause of chemical combining action, and explains why it should occur at all, for all bodies at heat disequilibrium must seek equilibrium. Hence in our study of chemical combining action, it is with this very latent-heat disequilibrium that we have started. We note, therefore, three kinds of latent-heat disequilibrium in chemicals :—1st, The latent-heat disequilibrium that chemicals may have with our earth ; 2d, The disequilibrium that they may have with our sun; 3d, The inter-chemical disequilibrium that chemicals may have with each other. When terric disequilibrium occurs, it is caused by our sun-heat coercing earth-force, as in oxygen and in water, vapour, &c. When solar latent-heat disequilibrium occurs, it is caused by the earth-force coercing the sun-force, and this is seen in free carbon. The inter-chemical latent-heat disequilibrium occurs between chemicals having different amounts of latent heat, as between free oxygen, nitrogen, hydrogen, and free carbon ; for the first three abound in sun-got latent heat, and the last, or free carbon, greatly lacks it. Further, this inter-chemical latent-heat difference or disequilibrium, or contrast or gap, is also greatly present between metals and metalloids,

since metals, by their conductivity, get during
certain chemical action latently earth cold; and
to metalloids combining with a metal, it thus
represents, during chemical action, our earth's
latent coldness or negativeness. This inter-
chemical latent-heat difference or disequilibrium
also exists, but in a varying degree, between
almost every chemical; so that sulphur is negative
to oxygen, but positive to selenium ; potassium is
negative to sulphur, but is positive to platinum,
and so on. And the greater this latent-heat difference between two elements, the greater their
latent-heat disequilibrium, and the greater their
tendency, *cæteris paribus*, to chemical combining
action ; and we always can make out this latent-heat
difference greatly between chemicals that readily,
violently, or in many ways combine. We see this
latent-heat difference well pronounced between free
carbon and oxygen, carbon and nitrogen, carbon and
hydrogen ; for carbon is an infusible solid, and oxygen, nitrogen, and hydrogen unliquefiable gases.
This great latent-heat contrast is seen between
metalloids and metals, seeing that to metalloids,
certain metals, even hydrogen itself, give always,
during action, our earth's latent coldness. This
remarkable latent-heat difference occurs between
the four organic elements, nitrogen and oxygen
on one side, and on the other hydrogen bound

to infusible carbon, as is mostly the case in organic
chemistry; for hydrogen is metallic, and has a
certain amount of conductivity and the greatest
known heat capacity, and hydrogen can thus, in
action with oxygen and nitrogen and carbon, give
the first two while taking also for itself carbon's
latent coldness.   Just as in mineral chemistry,
the common metals in action with metalloids
represent our earth's latent coldness, so hydrogen
in its organic actions with oxygen and nitrogen
represents to them carbon's latent coldness.   This
latent-heat difference is also seen between the
anhydrids and their acids, and the bases and so
on.   The law therefore is, that between chemicals
enjoying great powers of combination there exists
in esse or *in posse* the latent-heat difference.   But
it does not follow, however, that whenever there
is this latent-heat difference there will result
chemical combining action; for this latent-heat
difference between two chemical particles can
only produce a proclivity in them to chemical
action, but does not necessarily give them the
powers of acting, which consist in latent-heat
changes demanding in the two particles not latent-
heat difference alone, but heat capacity also.   If
the two particles have not the necessary heat
capacities they cannot act chemically together.
Between light, unliquefiably gaseous oxygen and

heavy and badly fusible platinum a very great
latent-heat gap exists ; and the consequent attraction, favoured as it is by the lightness and
mobility of gaseous oxygen, is seen between
them ; and the first step to chemical combining
action is taken by the free oxygen and platinum
thus attracting, but action proceeds no further; for
platinum has great weight and equivalent, and
thus too limited heat capacities to accompany
free, gaseous oxygen in the great latent-heat
changes it undergoes in oxyplatinal action, for
in this action unliquefiable oxygen, in partnership
with platinum, has to solidify. When you have
liquid, nascent, instead of free, unliquefiable oxygen, then oxyplatinal action occurs, for then the
latent-heat changes of liquid oxygen into solidity
are smaller, and better suit the small heat capacities of platinum.

CHAPTER V.

Nature of chemical combining action: first latent-heat difference
in chemicals leads to their attraction and molecular contact,
which then causes latent-heat discharges or changes in the
chemicals to produce their latent-heat equilibrium, at which
action stops: the latent-heat changes occasion the transformations of the action. Attraction important, but cannot
singly explain chemical combination. The several ways in
which latent-heat changes occur during combination, and the
equilibrium produced by them: their constant occurrence.
Causes of chemical transformations. Various latent-heat
equilibria attainable by combination. The latent-heat mean
of chemical combination.

CHEMICAL combining action therefore is complex,
and consists not of one action—attraction—only,
but of a series of actions. 1st, Latent-heat disequilibrium, causing chemical attraction and contact of two molecules, and the necessity for their
chemical action; 2d, After the attraction and
chemical contact of the two molecules latent-heat
changes in the molecules; leading to, 3d, Latent-
heat equilibrium of the two molecules; which
produces, 4th, The transformations correlated to
latent heat, and thus new compounded substances.
Attraction is therefore highly important in combination, and we see that it always must occur;

D

and, in fact, up to the present, attraction has had
all to do in the theory of chemical combining action;
but although attraction evidently does much in
that action, yet it is as clear that it does not do all;
for the chemists themselves always put the adjec-
tive " chemical " before attraction when used in
explanation of the phenomena of combination, and
this seems to prove that in chemical combination
there are residual phenomena which chemists are
conscious of, and which attraction alone fails to
explain; and these residual phenomena are the
latent-heat changes and equilibrium, with the correlated transformations.

Attraction in chemistry, therefore, does not differ
from that in physics, and but brings attracting
molecules into close apposition. This attraction
in chemistry is, however, a molecular force, and
has for its cause the difference of latent heat, heat
being an agent quite capable of acting on all molecules of all matter; and this latent heat we shall
anon find, by the study of the galvanic battery,
to be an electric phase of energy; hence chemical
attraction is subject to electric laws, and to com-
prehend it, the laws of electricity, galvanism, and
magnetism must be investigated. The latent-
heat changes of chemical combination, though
every whit as important and as constantly present
as its attraction, have been so little noticed in

chemistry that I shall be obliged to adduce some
explanatory instances of them. Gaseous oxygen
and hydrogen combine and produce liquid water;
in combining there has been a change of the
latent heat of the two gases by their passage
by combination into liquidity; there has been a
united latent-heat disoccupation by the two gases.
It is true that this latent-heat change has simul-
taneously occurred to united gases instead of to one,
but I do not see how this alters the case from the
latent-heat point of view. Free oxygen was a gas;
in liquid water, though united to hydrogen, in
what latent-heat state is oxygen? Is oxygen,
in liquid water, in the same latent-heat state as
when oxygen is free and gaseous? or has the free
gaseous oxygen in becoming liquid in water gained
latent heat? or has oxygen lost it? One of the
three must have happened; and we have the
most right to hold that gaseous oxygen in becoming, though accompanied by hydrogen, liquid in
water, lost or disoccupied latent heat, because this
conclusion is most in unison with all the analogous facts of science. Further, the two gases,
oxygen and hydrogen, have, as ingredients of water,
like latent heats; for the two in water solidify,
melt and vaporise together, and this similarity
is a latent-heat equilibrium. Again fluid mercury
and gaseous oxygen combine and form a solid—

the oxide of mercury; the two, therefore, in becoming the components of this solid oxide, must
have changed, or lost, or discharged, or disoccupied
their latent heats analogously to what oxygen
and hydrogen did; and the two also reach an
analogous latent-heat equilibrium, to be presently
examined more fully. Again, gaseous oxygen
and solid but fusible zinc combine and produce
a more infusible solid, the oxide of zinc; and
gaseous oxygen and fusible zinc, in becoming the
ingredients of the less fusible solid oxide of zinc,
changed or disoccupied their latent heats analogously to what oxygen with hydrogen, oxygen with
mercury, did; and further, the zinc and oxygen, in
their oxide, attained also the latent-heat similarity
or equilibrium. In all these three cases, a metal
and a metalloid were concerned, and we had latent
heat discharged from all the actors into surrounding matter—that is, eventually, to our earth, which
thus becomes, as we shall hereafter clearer find, the
great latent-heat centre of equilibrium for certain
chemical actions of mineral chemistry; that is,
the frequent common reservoir for our chemical
latent heat of minerals, analogous to what she is
well-known to be for friction or tension electricity.
Two solids, carbon and sulphur, powdered, mixed,
and heated, combine and form a liquid, the bisulphuret of carbon; the two solids, therefore, in

becoming components of their liquid bisulphuret,
changed their latent heats by taking it from the
fire by which the solids were heated; here, therefore, the solid combiners had latent heat, so to
speak, discharged into them instead of from them,
as we saw the case in oxymetallic combinations;
and further, the two, carbon and sulphur, reached
the usual latent-heat similarity or equilibrium.
Again, solid sulphur combines with unliquefiable
oxygen and produces a liquefiable gas—sulphurous
anhydrid, in which unliquefied oxygen became
liquefiable, and thus approached liquidity; and thus
discharged or lost latent heat and solid sulphur
gasified by receiving part of this heat; that is,
latent heat was transferred from the latently
hotter combiner oxygen to the colder sulphur, and
the ordinary latent heat-equilibrium was struck,
analogous to those of the ingredients of water, and
of the oxide of mercury and of zinc, and of the
bisulphuret of carbon. So that in direct, simple
chemical combining action, latent heat has several
courses in passing into equilibrium; each, however, easy to trace. 1st, Latent heat may be
equilibrised by being discharged or disoccupied
from, or by, both combiners, as in metallic oxidations. 2d, Latent heat may be equilibrised by being
taken from extraneous sources and occupied by
both combiners, as in the bisulphuret of carbon.

3d, Latent heat may be equilibrised by discharges
from one combiner into the other, as in sulphurous
anhydrid ; and lastly, in all chemical combinations
there results a latent-heat similarity and equilibrium between the combiners which requires fuller
consideration hereafter.   Nor is there a single
chemical union in which some of these latent-heat
changes and the final equilibrium are not found
to take place ; and we thus arrive at a law in
chemistry—namely, that chemical combination
always changes and equilibrises the latent heat of
combiners, by its loss or gain or transference.
This law is quite universal in chemistry.   But
these latent-heat changes must entail upon combiners the correlative changes of form also ; hence
a great number of the transformations that combining chemicals undergo become intelligible by
comparing these transformations to those that
familiar latent heat produces on matter.   Thus the
transformation of gaseous hydrogen and oxygen to
form water is made comprehensible by the statement that both simply lost their latent heat when
rushing together into union and mixture.   They
must have done so ; we even see that they do so ;
and this discharged heat has even been estimated
by St Clair Deville and Bunsen.   Surely the transformation by latent-heat change of invisible steam
into liquid water is, though familiar, as strange as

the analogous transformation of the two invisible
gases, hydrogen and oxygen, combining into liquid
water. The shapes of cloud, invisible steam, liquid
water, snow and ice, impressed by latent heat on
the oxide of hydrogen, are as remarkable, though
their effect on us be lessened by early and constant familiarity, as many of the chemical transformations. But latent heat influences the form
and aspects of chemicals in another manner—it
gives them allotropy. All chemicals that become
allotropic change their relations to latent heat—
occupy or disoccupy latent heat when they become
allotropic. Thus by heating, for some time, phosphorus in gases inactive to it, we come to change
its fusion point from being at 115° to 500°; that
is, we change the relations of phosphorus to latent
heat by making it recede from liquidity, and we
find that by so doing we also alter phosphorus'
shape and aspect, and it passes to the red variety
of phosphorus; and analogous results are obtained
with sulphur, and the compound red oxide of
mercury, and many other bodies. The transformations, therefore, of chemistry that are not
explicable by the agency of the common latent
heat, are easily so by that of the latent heat of
allotropy. That the common and allotropic latent-
heat changes, and no other agency, have the
necessary powers of form-alteration is certain;

that by chemical action latent heat is changed in
a way quite analogous to what happens in altera-
tion of state and during allotropisation, is also
evident. We therefore feel warranted in holding
that all chemical transformations are explicable
by referring them either to the action of common
or of sun-got or of allotropic latent heat, severally
or conjointly. A chemical compound is a mixture
of its components, but they have undergone, at
their combination, latent-heat changes, and are
therefore allotropic—have therefore new forms,
which are even possible for us, in a measure, to
foresee. When a chemical compound is viewed as
a mere intimate mechanically attracted mixture of
its components, it is inexplicable that the mixture
should not resemble the physical mean of the
things mixed. There is no such difficulty, however,
when we allow that a compound is a mixture of
ingredients that have, by latent-heat changes,
become allotropic or transformed ; for an irresis-
tible and competent transforming force, latent heat,
has acted in the ingredients of every compound,
and it is little wonder that they have yielded and
transformed. Hence latent heat in chemistry is
morphigenic force.

The existence, therefore, of the two great chemical forces, our sun and our earth, and the heat
constitution of matter, throw chemicals into latent-

heat disequilibrium with each other, or our earth
or sun; and this explains their chemical action at
molecular contact, since we know that chemicals
that are in latent-heat disequilibrium must strive
or be prone to attain equilibrium, which they do
by latent-heat changes or discharges; and these
also distinctly explain the transformations of chemical action and the production of new compounded
substances.   But it is also clear that latent-heat
changes in chemicals can alone take place according to their heat constitution, specially their heat
capacities; and this also explains the existence in
chemistry of action in equivalent, proportional
weights, for they inversely represent the chemicals' capacities for heat.   If chemical combining
action consist in latent-heat changes or discharges,
such discharges must be given and taken according to the powers that the givers and takers have
of giving and receiving latent heat; that is, according, as we have found, to the heat capacities
and conductivities of the heat-givers and takers.
In seeking latent-heat equilibrium by heat discharge or change, that is, in acting chemically,
every chemical is bound to act according to its
heat constitution or its powers of latent-heat reception or discharge.   Thanks to the labours and
the genius of such men as Dulong, and Petit, and
Regnault, &c., we have come to know that the

capacity for heat of chemicals is inversely as their
equivalents. Some such law might have been
expected, and is most important in a natural
theory of chemical action. We know, therefore,
that as the elements differ in their amount of
latent heat, they vary in their powers of being
affected by it; that is, the elements differ in their
capacities for heat, their equivalents, and their
conductivities. Some elements acquire and conversely discharge this latent heat with ease and
others with difficulty; and on this power will
greatly depend their chemical activities, and to it
constant reference will require to be made; for
no chemical action occurs without latent-heat
changes.

But even attraction and these latent-heat
changes, important and constant though they be
in chemical action, do not yet constitute its most
signal phenomenon, and are but means to an end
—steps for the attainment of a latent-heat equilibrium in all the factors in chemical action.
Latent-heat disequilibrium was the primary cause
of chemical combining action, and equilibrium its
end—latent-heat equilibrium of all the actors and
factors of the combination; and when this is
achieved, all action ceases for the equilibrised
chemicals, more or less permanently and completely, according, as we shall eventually see, to

the nature of the equilibrium obtained. As there
are various chemical latent-heat disequilibria, so
there are the correspondent latent-heat equilibria.
There is, first, an equilibrium in which our earth
preponderates, and which shall be termed the
terrestrial, or mineral, or inorganic. Our earth's
size, passiveness, considerable latent coldness, or
negativeness, heat constitution, pre-eminently fit
her to be for mineral chemistry the latent-heat
centre of equilibrium, or the common reservoir for
latent heat of acting chemicals, as she is known
to be for the electricity of tension. Secondly,
there is the organic equilibrium, in which carbon
plays an analogous part for organised compounds
to what our earth does for minerals : carbon being
the organic earth, the latent-heat centre of equilibrium for organic chemistry; for which carbon's
very great latent coldness or negativeness, heat
capacity and conductivity, amply fit carbon.
Thirdly, there is the equilibrium in which our sun-
force preponderates, as in living, breathing organ-
isms.   Fourthly, there are what might be called
the minor or intra-chemical equilibria, or those
which chemicals can afford to each other.   And
all equilibria might also be described to be an
assumption by all combiners of a similarity of
latent heat, consisting of a *mean* of *all the latent
heats primarily concerned, or secondarily implicated*

in the given combining action. This, to which
reference must often be made, shall be called the
latent-heat mean of combination, and by its
existence we shall yet see that some likeness
between chemical children and their parents can
at last be traced. If the chemical combining
action be confined merely to the two actors, or be
intra-chemical, then the latent-heat mean of
combination will be that of the two actors alone,
and the compound produced will have a latent
heat pretty much the mean of that of the two
actors, as in sulphurous anhydrid. If in the
combining action our earth's influence or chemical
forces enter, then in the latent heat of the compound our earth's latent heat and correlated form
appear, as seen in metallic protoxides called
" earths." If in the combining action our sun's
or fire's influence preponderates, then this will be
apparent in the final latent-heat mean of the
compound. So that, meditating on chemical combining action, we must have in mind the existence
of sun-got latent heat among chemicals, and the
disequilibria that its dissimilarity produces, and
the attraction and molecular contact and latent-
heat changes and final equilibrium in chemicals
that from it arise—the equilibrium being necessarily a balanced mean of all the latent heats

concerned; and it must be recollected that it is of latent heat we treat, for the appreciation of which not thermometers avail us, but certain correlated forms that this heat is known to give to matter.

CHAPTER VI.

Of chemical action in general; its latent-heat disequilibria, changes, and final equilibria. The division of chemical combining action into the great and minor actions; further subdivisions. Metal-lico-metalloid combinations; their nature, cause of their frequent violence: participation of our earth in such actions; the results of this seen in the forms and aspects of metallico-metalloid compounds, or in their latent-heat mean of combination. Reasons of nitrogen's chemical inactivity compared with oxygen. Of the nascent form, and the reasons that it facilitates combining actions. Of the nature of the combinations of hydrogen; intra-metallic combining action; cause of non-action between hydrogen and other metals. Intra-metalloid combining actions. The reasons of the difficulty of union between atmospheric oxygen and nitrogen.

CHEMICAL action may be divided into two great classes. First, the great, and, second, the minor actions. The great actions may be subdivided into two, the inorganic and the organic. For the inorganic actions our earth is the equilibric latent-heat centre, and both our sun and fire may take part. For the organic actions carbon is the equilibric latent-heat centre, and by its heat nature renders possible the existence of another chemical organic world within the larger mineral world, and where the sole heat-source is our sun; and the mineral and organic actions of chemistry are

great, just because of the perfection of their centres
of heat equilibrium.   The minor actions of chemistry take place between comparatively isolated
chemicals, and for such actions no great special
latent-heat equilibric centre exists, but several
minor ones that the chemicals may give to each
other; hence the minor actions of chemistry are
on a lesser and not so final a scale.

Before commencing the examination of chemical
action in detail, we must recapitulate, and again
point out that, for its comprehension, we must be
able to ascertain the amount of latent heat of
each of the actors; for by that alone we can
judge of their latent-heat differences, and consequently of their attraction and the strain put on
them to urge them to act.   We must also have
means of tracing the latent-heat changes or behaviour of the actors in chemical action, and in
their finally resulting latent-heat equilibria.   The
amount of latent heat in chemicals is known by
their weight and state, not by any means with great
exactitude, but sufficiently so for the necessities
of chemical theoretical research.   The latent-heat
changes of chemical action are discoverable by
attending to the heat capacities, weights, and
conductivities of the actors; the nature of the
final latent-heat mean of combination is seen by
considering all the phenomena of the action, taking

into computation not only apparent but secondarily
implicated actors, and by using form and certain
properties of matter correlated to latent heat as
its index or thermometer. To commence the
detailed study of chemical combining action we
naturally choose the simplest, and take direct
binary intra-elementary actions; and first of
metallic proto-metalloidations—that is, direct
binary combination of metals with metalloids.
There exist among the chemical elements two
classes—the metalloids, in which I include arsenic,
and exclude carbon, boron, silicon, and the metals.
The metalloids are light and non-conductive, and
comparatively heat capacious, and therefore slowly
take latent heat from our sun, and slowly give
heat away earthwards. Hence latent heat has, as
it were, time to delay or remain in metalloids,
and they become, in chemistry, magazines or
holders of latent heat; and if not gases, are, by
being volatile, near it, and are thus unlike the
typical solid form of our earth, and are in a position of constraint to our earth-force analogous to
that of water-vapour, and requiring to be retained
in that position perforce by sun-got or fire-got
latent heat. The metalloids of our earth being
at latent-heat disequilibrium, are urged by the well-
known heat constitution of both reciprocally to
strike an equilibrium, but the metalloids fail to do

so owing to their non-conductivity; for our earth can take the latent heat from metalloids only in its thermometric phase.

Metals all conduct heat, and are all good links for thermometric heat between the thermometrically hot and cold; but all metals are not good latent-heat links, because for that, in addition to conductivity, lightness and heat capacity are needed. Some metals are heavy and little heat capacious, as platinum, &c., and cannot thus be much affected by our sun, and remain in nature in shapes similar to that of earth matter reduced to a typical generality, and at earth equilibrium.' Metals that are light and heat capacious and conductive, as calcium, potassium, &c., are good latent-heat links, and sustain by heat or our sunforce alterations from the typical earth matter, and lose equilibrium with it, but to a less extent than the metalloids, and seek equilibrium less strongly than the metalloids. When a metalloid is single, therefore, though greatly wanting in terrestrial equilibrium, it lacks the conductivity necessary to attain it; the conductive and heatcapacious metal, however, singly lacks only the strong impulse to equilibrium. But highly earthdisequilibrised metalloid, and the conductive, heatcapacious metal in union, supply each other with the complete conditions of heat equilibrising with

E

our earth, and the three do act together; and in the metallic protoxide arising, lime, magnesia, the earth's latent heat and the correlated earth form enter. If we bring a latently hot metalloid, say oxygen, and a less latently hot heat-capacious metal, say potassium, and our vast latently cold earth, together into latent-heat relations, then the conductive potassium forms a centre of inductions. The latent heat that is in conductive potassium reacts inductively on that of oxygen, which reciprocates, and the latent heat of potassium also reacts on that of our earth, that also reciprocates. When we, therefore, put thus together metalloid, heat-capacious, conductive metal and our earth, we increase the amount of latent heat that aims at earth equilibrium; we add fourfold to what might be called the inductions, and we also give virtually to the metalloid metallic conductivity, and to the metal metalloidal great earth-disequilibrium; and thus augmenting quantity, tension, discharging powers of the actor's latent heat, we do bring about most violent action and earthward discharges. When oxygen, therefore, intimately touches potassium, there is at once violent and stable chemical combination, called combustion or burning; for in the combination of potassium and oxygen we have many things to produce readiness, violence, and stability

of action. We have the great disparity in latent
heat of the actors, which are virtually our solid,
rather infusible earth, and the extreme gaseity of
unliquefied oxygen; and further, we have the excellent latent-heat communication between them
furnished by conductive, heat-capacious potassium. There is thus for the action great pressure
put upon the actors, the solid earth and gaseous
oxygen, by their great latent-heat disparity; and
there is every facility of action afforded them by
the intervention between them of latent-heat
conducting potassium. Finally, the equilibrium
reached by the combination is in unison with
that of matter around or of our earth, and thus
stable; and also from the passage earthward in its
thermometric phase of the heat-force disoccupied
by the assumption of an earth-similitude or solidity, by hitherto solar gaseous oxygen, we have
the flash characteristic of combustion. The heat
that we see during metallic proto-metalloid action
was heat latent in the actors before action, and
obtained with more or less removes ultimately
from our sun, and occupied in giving certain anti-
terrestrial forms to the actors. Hence the result of
the action is to give to the actors concerned in
the compound produced an earth likeness, and
some of these compounds are so like the general
matter of the earth that they are styled "earths."

And this earth-like appearance in metallico-
metalloid proto-compounds must arise, since there
exists in every chemical combination not a physical, but an equilibric latent-heat mean, struck
between the latent heats of all the actors and
factors of the combining action. Now in all
metallico-metalloid direct proto-combinations our
earth's latent heat takes an essential part, and
thus must enter into the latent-heat mean of combination. But latent heat is correlated to form;
so that, with our earth's latent heat, her form is
also unavoidably taken. Therefore if our earth
intervenes in metallico-metalloid proto-compounds,
her presence should be indicated in their formulæ,
thus: E_xM, O, or a metallic protoxide; in which
E stands for our earth, and M for any directly oxidisable metal, and x for the part our earth takes, not
quantitatively known, and O for oxygen. And this
throws light on the organic hydro-carbon radicles;
for even in all metallic inorganic protoxides there
exists a radicle, E_xM, that cannot be isolated, corresponding to the often non-isolated hydro-carbon
radicles of organic oxides, which radicles are composed of carbon, the organic earth, or latently
negative latent-heat centre of equilibrium of
the conductive and very heat-capacious metal
hydrogen, thus, $C_{2n}H_{2n+1}$. In metallic proto-
metalloidations, therefore, there is the latent heat

of a latently hot metalloid discharged through a
metal into our earth, because she is latently cold ;
and hence that part of the earth, her magnetic
pole, which is the latently coldest, is what the heat-
discharging metal is thrown into closest latent-
heat relations with, and to which we shall see in
future, under certain circumstances, the metal will
turn or be magnetically attracted, and this gives
us the rudimentary idea of the causes of electro-
magnetism.   There are, therefore, four arguments
for holding that our earth intervenes in metallico-
proto-metalloidal actions : First, that the heat constitution of matter exists for nature as well as for
the laboratory, and will cause the actors to obey our
sun or our earth as representatives of heat and
cold ; second, we see that an assumption of more
or less earth-likeness by the actors is the characteristic of these actions ; third, we have the analogy
of the hydro-carbon radicle ; and lastly, the phenomena of electro-magnetism.

Let us reflect a little further on what is demanded of potassium or any suitable metal in
order to be oxidised.   Potassium is required to
receive and transmit earthward the latent heat of
oxygen and its own, for which both conductivity
and heat capacity are required in potassium.
There is always a definite amount of heat to be so
transmitted, and the heat capacity of potassium is

also definite, and strictly limited by its equivalent.
Now let us suppose that in these metallic protoxidations we increased the quantity of the heat
of all phases that oxygen has to send earthwards
through the metal, say potassium, in order to pro-
toxidise it; then it might well happen that the
potassic heat capacities strictly limited by its equivalent might no longer suffice for this now augmented amount of oxygenic heat, and consequently
no earthward passage of oxygenic latent heat
through potassium, nor consequently any chemical
action, could take place. This increase of latent heat
we actually produce when we substitute for oxygen
in the action a still latently hotter metalloid, as is
nitrogen. Both oxygen and nitrogen are unliquefied
gases, and we do not know which is the more unliquefiable; but we conclude that nitrogen is latently
hotter than oxygen, because nitrogen is lighter and
is more insoluble in water than oxygen; and thus
nitrogen is, with the sole exception of hydrogen,
the most latently hot or positive of all the elements.
But we find that nitrogen's equivalent, by which
its heat capacity is inversely measured, is nearly
twice that of oxygen, and fourteen times that of
hydrogen. Hence, if we try to produce, instead of
metallic oxidations, nitridations, we fail, for very
latently hot nitrogen, brought into contact with
metals, has, in order to combine with them, to

offer them more latent heat than oxygen, and than metals can take to transmit earthward; consequently the metals refuse terro-nitrogenic action. Nitrogen's own heat capacity is not great, considering the amount of latent heat it has to discharge; therefore nitrogen's own discharge of its great latent heat is already difficult, and encounters in metals a further difficulty of reception and earthward transmission. Accordingly the metals and nitrogen fail to act chemically; for without discharge of latent heat no chemical action can occur. Everything, therefore, that hinders or prevents heat discharge and acceptance impedes or destroys chemical combining action; and conversely, everything that facilitates latent-heat discharges and acceptance promotes or produces chemical combining action. The non-conductivity, the weaker heat capacities of nitrogen imprison, as it were, its great latent heat within it, and impair its chemical activity. Nitrogen's power of heat discharge does not correspond with the great amount of heat it has to discharge, nor with the powers of latent-heat acceptance of the generality of its brother chemicals. If, on the contrary, we substitute for latently hot unliquefied oxygen and nitrogen, in certain metallic combinations, a latently colder metalloid, liquefiable chlorine, or a latently colder form or allotropy of oxygen—

ozone—we shall find that we facilitate the action ;
and so chlorine and ozone attack certain chemicals
that common oxygen does not; for in these circumstances we have the actors in tho chemical
action in a latently colder state, and the consequent diminished amount of latent heat in the discharges does not require such high heat capacity
in the givers and takers of the discharge, that is,
in the actors of the chemical action, which is thereby facilitated. And these circumstances serve
also to explain to us the power of what is called
in chemistry the nascent form in promoting
chemical combination; for if it be the great latent
heat and comparative small heat capacity of free
nitrogen and of its associates that is one of the
causes that makes their chemical actions difficult,
then nitrogen should be got sometimes to act if
it had a less latent-hot form, as is the case in
nascent nitrogen and nascent chemicals in general,
for nascent chemicals are generally in the liquid
form. The rest of the metallico-metalloid chemical combinations, those between the halogens, sulphur, phosphorus, arsenic, and the metals, are perfectly analogous to oxymetallic actions ; the same
species of inductions and consequent latent-heat
discharges earthward from the acting metalloid
(which, at times, as in sulphur, requires to be
artificially heated) through a suitable metal, leading to an assumption of terro-metallico-metalloid

equilibrium; the amount and character of the
heat discharge, of course, differing with each acting
metalloid and metal. For example, the heat
discharges that liquefiable, and not very heat-
capacious chlorine, can throw into our earth during
its metallic combinations, can never be so great
as those that oxygen under similar conditions
would yield, for chlorine is latently colder and
less heat capacious than oxygen. Hence the
latent-heat mean struck by metallic chlorides with
our earth is not so latently cold as the mean of
the metallic oxides; the chlorides, therefore, are
not bases, but more resemble the mean of salts.

Our earth has, therefore, great influence on
the direct metalloidations of the common metals,
in virtue of her size, passiveness, and chemical
forces; but our earth's want of chemical contact
impedes this influence, since it diminishes with
distance, and so much is non-contact against our
earth, that it is only by her immensity that she
at all overcomes it. Now, among the metals,
there are some that have considerable weight and
equivalent, and the resulting chemical passiveness
and negativeness, and that are thus chemically
like our earth, but having the advantage over
her, that they can be brought into close contact
with chemical actors; so that these metals not
only can represent our earth in miniature, but
can, in certain chemical actions, supersede her.

The two gases, oxygen and hydrogen, may be kept
mixed without combination, for both being unliquefied gases, there is not much latent-heat
difference between them, and thus to induce their
mutual isolated combination there is little pressure
existing.   The cause of their violent and permanent union being their great terrestrial latent-
heat dissimilarity, which is in great measure
annulled by the non-conductivity of both, even of
hydrogen, though a metal, and by the earth's
distance.   But if in this gaseous mixture of
oxygen and hydrogen we put the very negative
metal platinum, we virtually place in close contact with the two gases our earth in miniature,
that is, however, near and acting also on miniature
amount of matter; that is, we complete the essentials of metallico-metalloid action.   We give to
oxygen, and imperfectly conductive hydrogen, a
better, because a nearer earth, platinum, needed
on account of the weak conductivity of hydrogen.
On the approach of platinum, oxygen and hydrogen
at once combine, that is, discharge heat; but the
hydrogen in this case cannot strictly burn, or give
its heat and oxygen's to our earth, because she
is superseded by a representative, the platinum,
which is the object that will take the heat of the
action, and will become red-hot.

Hydrogen being gaseous, though a metal, conducts

heat less perfectly than the other metals; hence it
is not bound to our earth by such a strong link as
the other metals are, and is thus able to escape
our earth's power frequently, though not always.
Between the three unliquefiable gases—oxygen,
nitrogen, hydrogen—the latent-heat difference
cannot be great; so that when hydrogen acts
with nitrogen or oxygen, reciprocal heat discharges
are difficult; and hydrogen's conductivity, though
imperfect, yet, as it is assisted by the peculiarity
of the case, allows our earth's influence upon
hydrogen, always present, to preponderate and to
attract, through hydrogen, earthward, the heat
discharges of the action, when water (HO) or
ammonia (NH$_3$) is formed. When, therefore,
hydrogen combines with oxygen and nitrogen to
form water and ammonia, all lose heat, which our
earth gains. And in the latent-heat mean of
combination, latently hotter nitrogen, with three
volumes of hydrogen, strikes a *gaseous* mean in
ammonia—that is, a mean higher than latently
colder oxygen, with two volumes of hydrogen,
does in *liquid* water. But when unliquefiable
hydrogen acts with easily liquefiable chlorine,
there is between them a greater facility of reciprocal heat inductions and discharges than there
was between hydrogen and nitrogen or oxygen;
for chlorine, being easily liquefiable, is not so

saturated with sun-got latent heat as unliquefiable
hydrogen, oxygen, and nitrogen; consequently,
when hydrogen unites with chlorine to form
hydrochloric acid, although our earth's influence
is still present, it does not preponderate, because
of the comparative facilities of chloro-hydrogenic
discharges, because of the contact of chlorine and
hydrogen and our earth's distance, because hydrogen's metallic earth link is not of the strongest.
Hence in the latent-heat mean of the combination
of hydrogen and chlorine in hydrochloric acid
our earth does not interfere, and it is a gas with
difficulty liquefiable, having the mean of its two
ingredients alone, unliquefiable hydrogen, and
easily liquefiable chlorine.

In hydrochloric acid there is, therefore, no
earth part at all, hydrogen then acting the *rôle*,
not of a metal, but of a very latently hot or
positive metalloid. Hydrogen, therefore, can act
in chemistry in two very oppositive manners—as
a metal or as a metalloid, as a negative or as a
positive, as an acidifier or basifier. With the halogens, sulphur, &c., hydrogen acts the metalloidal,
positive, latently hot, solar part, and forms acids.
With oxygen, and very latently hot nitrogen,
hydrogen acts as a metal, comes under our earth's
influence, transmits its own and oxygen's or nitrogen's heat earthward, and becomes thus latently

earth-cold, neutral in water, and basic in ammonia.

When hydrogen combines with the halogens, it
has to raise them into gases, the hydro-halogenic
acids; but to do this to the halogens, which are
gases, or by being volatile near it, hydrogen does not
require to give much latent heat, and unites with
halogens in equal volumes. But to combine with
sulphur, phosphorus, &c., hydrogen must raise
to the gaseous mean elements less volatile or
gasifiable than the halogens; and more volumes
than one of hydrogen are needed and taken in
these combinations of sulphureted and phosphoreted hydrogen.

For analogous but converse reasons phosphorus
and nitrogen take, in phosphoreted hydrogen and
ammonia, three volumes of hydrogen to combine
with; the phosphorus, because it is so latently
cold, that in order to gasify it requires great
latent heat; the nitrogen, because it is so latently
hot that it requires large amount of a heat-capacious metal to transmit earthward its great latent
heat.

As in the latent-heat scale, gaseous chlorine is
the hottest, and liquid bromine the next, and
solid iodine the last, the latent-heat mean of
combination that each strikes in the hydro-
halogenic acids, with one volume of hydrogen,

is in the same order latently colder and colder. You can solidify hydriodic acid with ease, hydrobromic with more difficulty, and hydrochloric acid has as yet not been solidified. The metals being more or less heavy, not very fusible or volatile solids, are not at great terrestrial latent-heat disequilibrium, and as they conduct heat, combining action, restricted to themselves, is facilitated and occurs, and our more distant earth does not interfere; and in the inter-metallic mean of combination, in alloys, resemblance even to the physical mean of the ingredients is generally observable.

Hydrogen does not combine with metals, because to transmit earthward, during action, free hydrogen's great latent heat, no metal's heat capacity suffices; for free hydrogen is more latently hot than even nitrogen; and to combine with hydrogen, independent of our earth, metals must strike an isolated latent-heat mean of combination with it—that is, with a very latently hot, light, and heat-capacious element; and metals so to do require to assume high solar, gaseous forms, for which, as a rule, their great weight, small heat capacity, and non-volatility quite unfit them. There are some metals, however, as arsenic, if it be indeed a metal, that, having volatility, can strike a latent-heat mean or can combine with hydrogen.

Nitrogen's chemical characteristic is its inactivity for mineral and activity for organic
actions. For nitrogen being very latently hot,
the heat capacities of the common metals and
metalloids, and of our earth herself, are not great
enough for the play of nitrogen's heat discharges;
and for nitrogen's actions a specially very heat-
capacious earth, carbon, and the most heat-capacious metal, hydrogen, conjoined with oxygen,
also very heat-capacious, have to be chosen; and
with such heat-endowed elements or associates,
nitrogen does act, and well; for it produces the
highest, the most complex chemical compounds
known—namely, those in organised beings. And
it is in truth the inorganic inactivity of nitrogen
that enables it to be *par excellence* the organisable
element—to be the chemical Prometheus, plucking
the fire of heaven to animate the minerals of the
earth into life. If we examine free oxygen and
nitrogen, we find them very permanently the
latently hottest matter on the earth, and latent
heat in these elements exists in the extremest
degree compatible with terro-solar equilibrium of
our matter. So that attraction and heat discharges are difficult between these two gases;
they are heat saturated already. Further, they lack
conductivity, and this is not only a difficulty to
their mutual union, but even to a heat discharge

towards our earth, to which they are at great
latent-heat disequilibrium. Further, nitrogen is
only moderately heat capacious, so that the two
gases lacking the necessaries of mutual isolated
chemical combination, namely, latent-heat difference, full heat capacity, and conductivity, never
directly unite, but remain the mechanically mixed
gases of our atmosphere. But sometimes these
two gases do unite with our earth, or the vapour
of water representing her; because for a terrestrial equilibration the two gases do possess greatly
one necessary condition, namely, a vast latent-
heat disequilibrium with our earth; and their want
of conductivity is annulled by a passage through
them and water vapour, earthward, of an electric
or lightning spark, in the wake of which, so to
speak, it is possible for their latent heat in immediate proximity, to a small extent, to pass
earthward, and thus liquid nitric be produced.
For the formation, therefore, of nitric acid from
free oxygen and nitrogen, the presence of moisture
or water vapour and the electric or lightning
spark are essential; for it is the water that
gives to the combining free oxygen and nitrogen
the possibility of a combinative equilibrium, that
is, the liquid nitric acid equilibrium, and the
electric or lightning spark, the possibility of reaching by 'heat discharge this equilibrium. Nitric

anhydrid is never formed under these circumstances, and is indeed a difficultly preparable,
that is, highly artificial substance, and very unstable, seeing that its sole ingredients, nitrogen
and oxygen, cannot furnish each other with a
perfect latent-heat balance, both being highly
solar and positive. In assuming this terrestrial
equilibrium with water, or in becoming liquid
nitric acid, free oxygen and nitrogen had to discharge considerable latent heat, for both became
fluid; and that ingredient, oxygen, which has
less heat to discharge and is latently colder, and
that is better at heat discharging, more heat
capacious, will take the preponderance in the
action or be in excess: so that nitric acid is composed of five equivalents of oxygen to one of
nitrogen (NO_5O, II).

The other compounds of oxygen and nitrogen,
namely, peroxide of nitrogen (NO_4), nitrous anhydrid (NO_3), nitric oxide (NO_2), and nitrous
oxide (NO), are derived from nitric acid and
nitrates by gradual ascent of the latent-heat scale,
and are never the result of direct mutual equilibrising heat discharges between free oxygen and
nitrogen. These compounds originate amid com-
plicated heat surroundings of concurrent chemical action, produced often by fire, which explains
their production. Again, as these compounds are.

F

formed by ascent of the heat scale, that component of them—nitrogen—that is the least heat-
capacious remains always the latently coldest, or
the negative part of the compound, although free
nitrogen be positive to oxygen. If we observe
oxygen, we find it heavier, more hydro-soluble,
more conductive, more heat-capacious, latently
colder than nitrogen. Further, in oxygen we see
also the power of even singly, in ozone, assuming
a more latently cold form—a greater earth-similitude; hence these are some explanations of the
greater chemical activity of oxygen over nitrogen.
Oxygen is an element whose amount of latent
heat, together with its heat capacity and conductivity and mass, render latent-heat changes between it and the rest of its fellow chemicals
generally practicable. Oxygen, by virtue of the
law of causation of chemical combining action,
will enter most readily into chemical action with
that metalloid between which and oxygen there
exists the greater heat difference and consequently
the greatest instability of latent-heat equilibrium,
always provided the heat capacity of that metalloid
be not insufficient; hence gaseous oxygen is known
directly to combine with sulphur, arsenic, phosphorus, in preference to chlorine, bromine, iodine.
Between gaseous chlorine and gaseous oxygen the
latent-heat disequilibrium is not so wide as be-

tween gaseous oxygen and solid sulphur. Nor is
chlorine's equivalent or heat capacity by half as
great as sulphur's; hence the absence of direct
action between chlorine and oxygen, and its
presence between sulphur and oxygen, might be
explained. The disequilibrium between gaseous
oxygen and liquid bromine and solid iodine is
great; but, then, the heat capacities and conductivities of these two last are small, and thus
may explain the non-occurrence of direct action
between them and oxygen.

Between oxygen and sulphur, both conducting
heat badly, direct chemical combining action
readily occurs, because both disequilibrium and
heat capacity greatly favour it; but the non-
conductivity of the actors isolate the action, and
we find in the sulpho-oxygenic compound formed,
in the sulphurous anhydrid's latent-heat mean, a
liquefiable gaseous shape midway between the two
equivalents of unliquefiable oxygen and the one
of the volatile solid sulphur. In sulphurous
anhydrid, which is a gas liquefiable by two atmo-
spheres, a solid ingredient, sulphur, has gasified,
and a highly gaseous one, oxygen, has all but
liquefied; that is, something of a mean has been
taken between high gascity and volatile solidity,
the gas oxygen and the solid sulphur being alone
concerned in the action. When oxygen combines

with phosphorus, the action is not, owing to the
better conductivity of phosphorus, so isolated to
the actors merely, and some heat must pass earthward; for in the phosphoric anhydrid produced we
have not the mean of the forms of the two ingredients—five equivalents of gaseous oxygen and
one of solid phosphorus, which mean would be
gaseous like sulphur's mean; but we have the
phosphoric anhydrid, a not very volatile solid.
That waxy phosphorus has the power of earthward
heat-discharge, we observe in it during its
assumption of the red allotropy of phosphorus.
For in passing from its waxy to its red state,
phosphorus changes its melting point from 111°
to 500°, and thus must become correlatively
latently specifically colder, liker to our earth, and
this could happen only by earthward heat-discharge on the part of phosphorus. A similar
earthward heat-discharge takes place during
oxyphosphoric action, and is seen in the latent-
heat mean of combination of the anhydrid formed.
The combinations of oxygen with its fellow-metal-
loids give rise to the oxyanhydrids, which shall be
fully discussed when we treat of acids and bases.
We have thus very imperfectly described certain
chemical actions in the equilibrium mean of which
our earth formed part, and also some actions
in which the equilibric mean was merely intra-

chemical. Sometimes, however, the sun, or its
representative fire, preponderates or influences the
equilibric mean of certain chemical actions, as
when, for example, the two solids, sulphur and
carbon, are together heated into combining into
the liquid bisulphuret of carbon. In this and
suchlike combinations, in the equilibric mean of
which fire predominates, the combiners, sulphur
and carbon, are heat capacious and one of them
carbon conductive; and it is the carbon, infusible
when free, that, by becoming in the bisulphuret
of carbon a volatile liquid, has most changed
latent heat and form, just because carbon is much
the more heat capacious and is conductive, and is
also in contact with a heat capacious, light, volatile, solid element, sulphur, by which carbon can
escape the trammels of our earth's influence.

CHAPTER VII.

The four organic elements, their heat-nature is the cause of their great chemical powers. Of the uses of carbon in organic chemistry. The latent-heat mean of chemical combination often beautifully apparent in organic compounds and others.

WHEN we consider chemical organic compounds, we are at once and greatly struck by their vast multitude, and still more so by the paucity of their components. The majority of the compounds of organic chemistry are formed of only two or three, or at most four ingredients; and this argues the greatest of chemical combining powers in these kingly elements. If chemical powers, therefore, consist in amount, difference, capacity, conductivity of heat proportioned to mass, then these heat endowments must be present and vividly apparent in the four organic elements. Of the four elements—nitrogen, oxygen, hydrogen, carbon—nitrogen and oxygen are the latently hottest in nature, being the unliquefied gases of our atmosphere, and carbon and hydrogen are also capable in composition of the highest of latent heats, as in carbureted hydrogen and carbonic acid and oxide; and it is a suggestive fact, that

all the four organic elements exist as gases—that
is, solar chemicals, in the atmosphere: nitrogen
and oxygen free, hydrogen as ammonia and water
vapour, carbon as carbonic anhydrid. There can,
therefore, be little doubt as to the amount of
latent heat that these four organic elements do
and can hold. The latent-heat difference between
these elements is also remarkable. Carbon free
is the most latently cold of the elements; the
latent-heat difference between infusible carbon
and the other three unliquefiably gaseous organic
elements, hydrogen, nitrogen, and oxygen, could
not therefore be greater. Further, between this
carbon and our earth there exist, as we said, heat
relations of an intimate nature. But further,
though there be great latent-heat difference between free carbon and free hydrogen, still this
difference may, from the conductivity and great
heat capacity of hydrogen and carbon, be between
the two easily effaced, and hydrogen thus forms
a perfect link between carbon and our earth on
one side, and oxygen and nitrogen and our sun
on the other. On the one side, therefore, we
have the great negative gradations of hydrogen,
carbon, and our earth; and on the other side, we
have the high positive gradations of oxygen,
nitrogen, and our sun. On the part of carbon,
we have mass, heat capacity, conductivity, pecu-

liarly suitable for terrestrial influence; on the
part of carbon and hydrogen, there is reciprocal
fitness of heat capacity, mass, and conductivity;
and on the union of carbon and hydrogen, in
radicles, we have mass, heat capacity, and extreme latent-heat coldness or negativeness, precisely requisite to balance the extreme latent heat
or positiveness of nitrogen and oxygen, and to
modify and multiply heat discharges between
them.

So that the sun-force and earth-force, in organic
chemistry, are much modified by passing through
these four links, nitrogen, oxygen, hydrogen, and
carbon; and it must be so, for in order to combine
gradually, by short heat stages, so to speak, the
four organic elements must be greatly withdrawn
from the direct chemical or heat influence of our
very powerful earth, and of fire or powerful sun.
When carbon, hydrogen, oxygen, and nitrogen
are free, the first two are, in *esse* or *posse*, very
latently cold, and the two last very latently hot;
and then to combine with each other, carbon and
hydrogen being conductive, the four must strike
an isolated latent-heat mean of combination; and
to get an isolated mean restricted to such latent-
heat extremes as theirs when free, requires large
latent-heat discharges and acceptance; and such
are difficult, and can occur only with the assist-

nnce of great forces, as our earth or fire, which
is a sun nearer and stronger than natural. So
that organic elements, when free, combine by the
great direct pressure of our earth or fire, and
discharge greatly and violently, and thus have
correlatively to assume extreme forms with their
extreme latent-heat discharge. Hence these four
organic elements, if free, cannot readily by
chemists be brought directly to produce organic
compounds; for the forces wielded by chemists—
fire and our earth—are far too violent in their
direct heat actions to give to actors the delicate
shades of latent-heat changes necessary to the
formations of organic compounds. But there
exists an organic territory on the earth, and of
this territory carbon is the latent-heat equilibrium
centre, and hydrogen the multiplier, modifier, and
transmitter of heat-discharges, and the distant
equable sun, through oxygen and nitrogen, the
sole heat-source. The presence of this, in a
measure independent kingdom, enables the organic elements to work undisturbed by the
grosser earth and fire, and controls the heat
phenomena and agencies, so as to produce moderate heat-discharges and the delicately heat-
balanced organic compounds. The possibility,
therefore, of the two kinds of chemistries—the
inorganic and organic, is owing to the existence

in nature of two great and perfect centres of latent-heat equilibrium—the latently cold earth, and the latently colder carbon; the source of latent-heat disequilibrium disturbance being also double—namely, the sun and fire.

With our large, passive, less heat-capacious earth, the sun or his metalloids, generally aided by fire, necessarily works in a very different way, and with other chemical tools from those he uses in working on light, heat-capacious, conductive, latently cold, morphigenic carbon. To act chemically with our negative, passive earth, and further with fire for his ally, the sun takes any metalloid, and even the latently colder of the metals, though not the best of heat transmitters; for the heat discharges that the sun or fire then, through metalloids and metals, gives, and that our passive, powerful earth then takes, are easy, being tensified, unmorphigenic electroid, and by these discharges, probably, the greater part of even the material earth has been fashioned. To work with heat-capacious, latently cold carbon, the sun, never assisted by fire, requires the very best of chemical workers, the most heat-perfect of the elements, the metalloids oxygen and nitrogen alone, and the best of heat transmitters—light and heat-capacious metallic hydrogen; for the distant sun-discharges are not violent, but moderate, and are going, not into a chemically passive, large object, as was our earth, but into light, heat-capacious, morphigenic, negative carbon. We see, therefore, in organic chemistry, the most equably and perfect of heat-sources—the sun alone —chosen and used; we see the best of chemical material—carbon—picked out, and the best of heat-transmitters—hydrogen—and the best of the heat-holders, nitrogen and oxygen. Hence the organic actions become thus the most perfect in chemistry, since in organic actions the forces, the material, and the instruments are the *élite* of chemistry; and from the heat actions of these four most perfectly heat-constituted elements the organic world in all its magnificence has undoubtedly arisen. If we sum up the heat capacities of the four organic elements, we find them far greater than the sum of those of any other four elements; and while all these four elements can exist as unliquefied gases, two also can exist in the opposite extreme of infusible solidity—carbon free and oxygen, in lime, &c.; and although nitrogen and hydrogen never descend the latent-heat scale so as to become so latently cold as to be infusible solids, still it is quite intelligible that even this may be absolutely necessary to keep up a certain degree of heat in the organised beings that these organic elements produce. The conductivity pre-

sent in carbon and hydrogen leads also to the
very important results, in addition to the facilities to heat actions that such conductivities con-
fer—namely, to these conductivities confining
and limiting the actions to the actors themselves;
hence organic actions have the impress or latent-
heat mean of combination, not of our earth, but
of the four elements themselves, and thus the
actions are organic, and not territorial or mineral.

Passing, however, from generalities into details,
let us proceed to compare inorganic with organic
protoxidations. The two are analogous. The
heat-source, our sun, through oxygen, is the same
in both; but in inorganic chemistry, fire or the
near sun is often used. And for the two the
equilibric heat-centre differs, our earth being the
inorganic centre, and carbon the organic, from
which is deducible the great dissimilarity in
aspect and nature of the two chemistries.

During a mineral, metallic protoxidation, we
have three things always concerned: namely, 1st,
A latently hot unequilibrised element—oxygen;
2d, A latently cold element, a centre of heat-equilibrium—our passive earth; 3d, Their connecting
link, the heat-transmitting metal—let it be in this
case hydrogen; and in the protoxide equilibrium
taken—in this case water—our earth virtually,
morphically forms a part. In fact, an inorganic me-

tallic protoxide must be considered, if the organic
protoxide is to be understood, as a combination,
not of two, but virtually of three objects—namely,
oxygen, metal, and our negative earth; and thus
formulised $E_x M_1 O$: in which E stands for
our negative earth, and x for the part she takes
in the action not quantitatively known, M for the
metal, and O for oxygen. A radicle, therefore,
$E_x M$, exists even in an inorganic, metallic
protoxide, only it can never be isolated, and is
seen by the assumption in that protoxide of an
earth-like shape. The part taken in inorganic
protoxidation by our earth (E) may be represented by x, as being as yet not quantitatively
known, but we see that this part, or x, varies in
amount, being greatest in the protoxides of the
earthy metals. In these inorganic, metallic protoxide radicles represented by the formula $E_x M$,
our earth therefore morphically exists; for her
latent heat, or virtual presence, is there seen in
the form or the state of the protoxide, and is thus
visible, comprehensible, admissible; and if so, we
at once get the clue to the nature of organic
protoxidation and the hydro-carbonic radicles.
For in the organic analogues of inorganic protoxidation we have also the same three objects—
namely, 1st, The latently hot unequilibrised oxygen; 2d, The latently cold infusible object, the

centre of heat-equilibrium, the morphigenic, light,
heat-capacious carbon; and 3d, Their connecting
link, the metal hydrogen. And we have a radicle
($C_{2n}H_{2n+1}$) (the general old notation formula for
various hydrated, organic protoxides, or various
monobasic alcohols) in which carbon, unlike our
earth, exists present, not only to logical or morphic, but also to chemical analysis, for so carbon's
chemical powers distinctly permit. And to take
a particular case, the hydrated oxide of methyl,
methyl alcohol (C_2H_3O+HO), we can decipher the
meaning of its formula only by comparing it to
that of inorganic protoxidation—namely, E_xH_1, O,
and then we see that organic protoxidation throws
light upon the inorganic, and *vice versa;* both
essentially consisting in equilibrising heat-discharges, passing through a suitable metallic link
from a latently hot unequilibrised element, oxygen, into a latently cold object, acting as a heat-
equilibric centre, our earth or carbon. But it is
clear that the nature and amount of these equilibrising heat-discharges will differ, according as
they are demanded from oxygen by our negative
earth or by negative carbon. For organic carbon—
that is, carbon with hydrogen—will demand for
protoxidation from oxygen far more morphigenic
heat than, under similar circumstances, our earth
will. Why? Because carbon is much lighter,

more heat capacious, latently colder, more morphigenic, and nearer the actors than the earth.
Hence we find in the formula of organic hy-
droxides one metal alone—hydrogen—that is
very heat capacious can be chosen. When water
is formed one equivalent of oxygen and hydrogen
are taken, for that hydrogen is sufficient to carry
earthward the quantity and tension of the heat
that oxygen gives, and our earth demands, while
inorganic water ($E_x H_1 O_1$) is forming.

But while methyl alcohol ($C_2 H_3 O + HO$), which
is an hydrated organic protoxide (an organic
water), is being formed, carbon demands of oxygen
more heat of untensified morphigenic phase than
our earth did, and it thus takes more hydrogen to
transmit carbonwards that heat. Hence the organic
waters, the monatomic alcohols, are of a latently
hotter type than common or inorganic water.
The organic compounds tend to be of a latently
hotter nature than the inorganic, for they are made
exclusively of the latently hottest elements, in
esse or *posse*, and the heat is always greatly
retained in carbon by morphigenesis. It is also
quite intelligible why neither the inorganic
($E_x M$) nor the organic ($C_{2n} H_{2n+1}$) radicles are
isolable and stable. The isolated existence of the
inorganic radicle, $E_x M$, is intelligibly impossible,
and that of the organic radicle, $C_{2n} H_{2n+1}$, may not

be altogether impossible, for the chemical affinities
of carbon and hydrogen are most perfect, but is
still difficult. Both such organic and inorganic
radicles represent, as it were, the half of an equilibrium. The carbon and hydrogen, the earth and
hydrogen, exist in union in such radicles, on account
of the presence of a third element, oxygen ; and if
that third element be taken away, the carbon and
hydrogen, the earth and hydrogen, in radicles, tend
also at once to part company, for their equilibrium
is destroyed. If we substitute hotter nitrogen for
oxygen, if we try to produce, instead of oxidation,
nitridation, we modify greatly the organic and
the inorganic actions. Everything indicates that
nitrogen is latently hotter than oxygen. So latently
hot is nitrogen, that it takes three equivalents
of the most heat - capacious of metals—hydrogen, when ammonia is formed ; that is, when
hydro-nitridation occurs, and the heat of one equivalent of unliquefied nitrogen is conveyed, through
hydrogen, into the earth, and easily liquefiable
ammoniacal gas produced. Now if nitrogen is so
latently hot as to require three equivalents of the
most heat-capacious of metals to convey earthwards its heat during hydro-nitridation, it becomes
intelligible that for nitridation no other metal's
heat capacity will suffice except hydrogen's ; and
the difficulty of combination of nitrogen with the

common metals receives some sort of explanation.
We have therefore our earth receiving the latent
heat of unliquefiable nitrogen, through hydrogen,
when easily liquefiable ammonia is formed; and thus
there is for ammonia a radicle, and in this radicle
there is an earth part, corresponding to every equivalent of metal, so that ammonia's formula is thus
written: $(E_{3r}H_3)N$. So that in ammonia there is
three times as much earth as there is in water, the
oxide of hydrogen $(E_x H)O$. So that ammonia is
basic, and more allied to the terrestrial or negative
bodies than water, which is neutral. In ammonia
four very hot unliquefied bodies—viz., one equivalent of nitrogen and three of hydrogen—have by
earthward discharge almost reached liquefaction,
whereas in water, only two hot unliquefied bodies—
one equivalent of oxygen and another of hydrogen
—attained by an analogous discharge liquefaction.
Hence heat discharges are greater and more difficult in ammonia, and it is not so easily formed as
water.

If we examine organic nitridation, that is, the
organic ammonias, we find that they are perfectly
analogous to the inorganic ones, and we have only
to substitute, in the organic ammonia, carbon—the
organic centre of heat equilibrium—for our earth,
which is the inorganic heat equilibrium centre. In
the inorganic ammonia radicle, the hydrogen is bound

G

to our earth, $E_{s_1}H_3N$; in the organic radicle, hydrogen is bound to carbon $(3(C_4)3(H_s))N$, triethylamine; and as in both the inorganic and organic ammonias, the nitrogen, the latently hot object, is in the minority, and the earth or carbon, the latently cold object, in excess of three to one, both the inorganic and organic ammonias tend to be latently negative or bases.

When we examine the four chemical elements—carbon, hydrogen, nitrogen, oxygen—that are almost alone employed in organic chemistry, we find that their combinations are peculiarly fitted to show the important law of the assumption of some sort of latent-heat mean of the combining chemicals by the same when combined; for of these four elements, two—nitrogen and oxygen—are of an extremely latently hot nature, and the other two —carbon and hydrogen—are in *esse* and *posse*, either naturally, or by easy heat transmission of an extreme latent coldness; tho two last, also, conducting heat. So that these two pairs of elements are nicely adapted to heat-balance each other.

Further, since carbon and hydrogen conduct heat, the chemical action and the combination heat mean can be greatly confined to merely these four elements. We know, therefore, that carbon and hydrogen will generally represent the latently cold objects in certain organic compounds, and that, *per contra*, nitrogen and oxygen will personify the latently hot nitrogen, being the latently hottest. For free carbon's relation to latent heat is that you cannot liquefy it; in other words, carbon's terrestrial nature is one prone to the utmost solidity. Free oxygen's relation to latent heat is the opposite of carbon's, for you cannot solidify free oxygen; nay, you cannot even liquefy it; for oxygen's free nature is one prone to the utmost gaseity. If we bear ·in mind these facts, we shall understand not a few of the heat means of combination in organic chemistry.

In the series of monatomic alcohols, the compound of oxygen and carbon plus hydrogen— methyl-alcohol (C_2H_3O+HO)—that has the least of the latently cold object carbon (C_2) and hydrogen (H_3), and thus relatively the most of the latently hot object oxygen (O), is a liquid boiling at 60° Cent.; that is, this liquid methyl-alcohol's proximity or proneness to gaseity—its oxygenic nature, in fact—is representable by its boiling point, 60° Cent. Let us, however, take Decatyl-alcohol ($C_{20}H_{21}O+HO$), in the same alcohol series, with ten times the carbon (C_{20}) that methyl-alcohol had (C_2), but the same oxygen, and we find Decatyl a liquid boiling, not at 60°, but at 212°; that is, liquid Decatyl's proximity or proneness to

gaseity, its oxygenic nature, representable by its
boiling point, 212°, is far less than methyl's, which
was 66°; for in Decatyl latently cold carbon (C_{20}) preponderates, if compared with methyl (C_2), in which
oxygen, so to speak, prevails. Methyl has less of
the latently cold object carbon, and thus relatively
more of the latently hot object oxygen, than Decatyl; hence methyl has more of the oxygenic
nature. Gaseity is easier to it than to Decatyl, for
methyl becomes a gas at 66°, and Decatyl only at
212°.

If we now, still further to increase the latently
cold object, carbon, in the same alcoholic series,
take melyl ($C_{60}H_{61}O+HO$), we no longer get a liquid
alcohol, but a solid one ; for we have augmented
so much the latently cold object carbon, that the
compound or alcohol has taken a mean of a greatly
latently cold nature, and become like the preponderating latently cold ingredient, carbon, solid.
Such, then, is the likeness that chemical offspring
bears to its progenitors ; for in this series of
alcohols, as the latently cold objects, carbon and
hydrogen, increase, the boiling or melting points
of the alcohols rise also, and that with the utmost
exactitude and regularity. The alcohols with
much carbon forsake gaseity or oxygenic nature,
and approach solidity or carbonic nature. The
forms of chemical compounds, therefore, bear a

definite, appreciable relation to the forms all their
ingredients have when free ; for chemical combination consists of an assumption of an equilibric
mean of all the latent heats concerned in the
combination and latent heat and form, and are
the reciprocal index of each other. In organic
chemistry, in the monatomic alcohols, in organic
protoxidation, this is strikingly seen, for in them
we have all the ingredients before our eyes, and
nothing but the ingredients are implicated in the
action. In inorganic chemistry, in the inorganic
metallic protoxidation, we have remarked that
this is also distinctly to be noted, if we recollect
that the metals are in chemistry transmitters of
heat ; that is, metals take and give heat readily
at any powerful demand. Hence metals must take
heat at the bidding of the latently hot metalloids,
and must yield it up at the command of our
latently cold earth ; and thus, on metallic metalloid-
ation, our earth, metal, and metalloid get mixed
up in the combination, and in it the form of our
earth appears very distinctly. In the compound
organic ammonias the same law is also distinctly
seen. In methylamine $(C_4H_8)+H+H)N$, the boiling point is below zero ; in octylamine $(C_{18}H_{17})+$
$H+H)N$, where we see the same amount of the
latently hot object nitrogen, but a great increase
of the latently cold object carbon + hydrogen,

boiling or assumption of gaseity has become more difficult, and takes place only at 170°.

The same law still holds good in the secondary and tertiary monamines. In the case of the monatomic alcohol's series, and the three kinds of monamines, the latently hot ingredient, oxygen and nitrogen, remain unchanged, and only the latently cold ingredient, carbon and hydrogen, suffer increase. But it must be evident that if we substitute for the latently hot object of the combination—that is, for oxygen and nitrogen—a less latently hot object, say phosphorus, we must also correspondingly affect the heat mean or equilibrium of combination. We must produce a latently colder combination, *cæteris paribus*, a compound more difficult to boil or to make a gas of. Hence we find that the phosphoric and arsenic organic bases have higher boiling points than the exactly corresponding nitrogen bases, because phosphorus and arsenic are solids, and thus latently colder than nitrogen, which is an unliquefiable gas. The nitrogen base, triethylamine, $3(C_4H_5)N$, boils at 91°; the phosphoric base, exactly corresponding to it, and called triethylphosphine, $3(C_4H_5)P$, boils at 127°5; and the antimonial corresponding base, triethylstibine, boils at 158°5, for antimony is even latently colder than phosphorus. Further, the nitrogen base, trimethyla-

mine, boils at 4° to 5°, and the exactly analogous
arsenical base, trimethylarsine, boils at 120°. The
olefine series show the same law. In these hydro-
carbons, hydrogen acts the part of a latently hot
metalloid, that is, the positive part, and carbon
the negative; and the boiling points of the olefines,
in series, become more and more difficult; the
assumption of a latently hot gaseous form becomes
harder and harder, with the increase in the olefines
of the latently cold object carbon. For although
the equivalents of carbon and hydrogen in olefines,
in series, always increase alike, the ratio of increase
by weight is for carbon by six, and for hydrogen
by one, so that the ratio of increase comes to be
very much in favour of carbon. As the latently
cold component carbon, therefore, multiplies much
faster in the series of olefines than the latently
hot hydrogen, the olefines, in series, assimilate
themselves to carbon's nature, and forsake that
of hydrogen, leave behind gaseity and approach
solidity.

In the series of monatomic alcohols, the latent-
heat discharge passed through hydrogen into
gradually augmenting carbon; and as latently cold
carbon alone increased, the latent-heat mean of the
alcohols, seen in their forms, forsook gaseity and
approached, and at length reached, a gradually
more and more infusible or insoluble solidity.

The liquid alcohols, in series, as latent-cold and very solid carbon was increased in them, became difficult to boil or to make gases of, and eventually they even became solids more and more difficult of fusion, when a maximum amount of their ingredient carbon was attained.

But let us choose compounds in which the latently hot ingredient, and not the latently cold one, is gradually increased. A latently hot element, chlorine (for its nature, when free, is gaseous), forms in gradually rising proportions, with the same amount of a latently cold element, carbon, a series of compounds, the subchloride (Cl_4C), the protochloride (ClC), the sesquichloride ($Cl_{1\frac{1}{2}}C$), and the bichloride (Cl_2C); and the latent-heat mean of combination in these compounds rises also with the quantity of chlorine they contain : the subchloride of carbon (Cl_4C) with the least chlorine, and thus virtually the most carbon is, like free carbon's latent-heat nature—solid.

The protochloride (ClC), with double the chlorine (a whole equivalent), is a liquid with a propensity to hotter form, representable by its boiling point, 248°. The bichloride (Cl_2C), with double the amount of chlorine that the protochloride had, is a liquid far more prone to hotter form, to become gaseous, than the protochloride, for the bichloride boils at 172°. The common sesqui-

chloride ($Cl_{11}C$) alone seems, at first sight, to
form an exception, for it contains half an equivalent of hot chlorine more than the protochloride
(Cl_1C) ; yet the common sesquichloride is a solid,
and the protochloride is a liquid.   It ought to be
the reverse.   But this depends upon the heat surroundings of the ingredients when the sesquichloride is formed.   These heat-surroundings, de-
pendent in this case on concurrent chemical action,
as in the case of the bisulphuret of carbon, take part
in the action, and so modify discharges as to alter
the final equilibrium of the common sesquichloride
of carbon.   But what proof is there of this ?   The
following :—Regnault obtained a liquid, isomeric
sesquichloride of carbon, by altering the heat-
surroundings of its ingredients at the time of
their combination.   Of the two gases, carbonic
anhydrid (CO_2) and carbonide oxide (CO), the
last (CO) is the latently hotter, being unliquefiable,
while the first (CO_2) is liquefiable ; yet the latently
hotter carbonic oxide (CO) contains less of the
latently hot element (O) than the carbonic anhydrid
(CO_2) ; but this is because when carbonic oxide is
formed there is always present around it sufficient
artificial heat to explain carbonic oxide's assumption of a high latent-heat state, carbon being very
heat capacious.   The discharges that raised carbonic oxide's latent-heat state came from without,

or from fire. In the reduction of certain metallic oxides by carbon and fire, we can produce, at will, carbonic oxide by raising the heat, or carbonic anhydrid by lowering it.

So that apparent exceptions to the law of the assumption of some latent-heat mean of chemical combination may be explained away by attending to all the phenomena of the exceptional cases.

CHAPTER VIII.

Of chemical affinity. Nature of combustion : relations of burning
metals to the earth's latent heat : the first glimpse of the
nature of galvano-electro-magnetism.

CHEMICAL combining action is, therefore, made up
of attraction and latent-heat changes, and final
latent-heat equilibrium of the actors.

Chemical affinity between two chemicals will
depend on the amount of their capabilities of
satisfying these conditions of combining action,
the attraction for combination demanding a latent-
heat difference between the actors. And in these
are often implicated and included our earth and
fire or sun ; the latent-heat changes for combination necessitating heat capacities and conductivities ; and its final latent-heat equilibria,
involving powers of assuming the latent-heat
mean of combination. Without the aptitude of
more or less fulfilling these conditions, no chemical affinity between two chemicals can exist. All
these three motions of chemical combination—the
attraction, heat changes, and equilibria, follow
each other in the very rapid sequence of an

electrical action, to which chemical combination is
most strictly correlated. If there were no difference of latent heat between two chemicals (including among such our earth), there could be
no attraction, nor consequently heat discharge,
nor heat equilibrium, nor transformation, nor
action between them at all.

In all chemical combining actions this latent-
heat difference between the actors, if you include
our earth and fire among such, is discoverable, and
exists as a necessary consequence of the heat-con-
stitution of chemical matter. Between chemicals—
including among such our earth—having the
greatest latent-heat difference, there exists the
greatest attraction; as in inorganic chemistry,
between unliquefiable oxygen and calcium bound
to our great solid earth; and as in organic
chemistry, between unliquefiable nitrogen and
oxygen, and hydrogen bound to infusible carbon.
And as latent heat is by the study of galvanism
resolvable into electricity, this attraction in
chemistry is electric; hence, from its electric
nature, chemical combination is dualistic; for
there must always exist in that action a positive
and a negative actor.   In the binary metallico-
metalloid compounds the metalloids are the positive actors, chiefly because of their small mass
and non-conductivity, and, besides, very general

good heat capacity; and the metals the negative actors, because of their greater mass and less heat capacities, but more because of the metals' conductivity, which in action produces a ready assumption by metals of earth-negativeness. In chemical combining action of metal and metalloid, therefore, the metalloids represent our sun, and the metals our earth; that is, the first, the positive, and the second, the negative actors. In compounds, not of elements, but of two compounds —for example, in acids—it is the acid's radicle, chiefly composed of metalloids, that represents the positive pole of the compound; and the metal hydrogen, with its earth connection, the negative pole of the compound. In salts it is the acid's radicle that is positive, and the metal with our earth that is negative. It does not affect the argument that some or many of these radicles are not isolable, for the existence of radicles is a polar one, often possible to them only as ingredients of compounds.

In organic compounds the same negative and positive polarity is clearly traceable, if we substititute for metal and our negative earth the metal hydrogen, negative by its carbon contact and union, oxygen and nitrogen being always the positive ingredients. What then is chemical affinity?

The prevailing idea would make it an inexpli-
cably mysterious force that will produce between
two chemicals at once, on the slightest contact,
direct, easy, violent, with difficulty decomposable,
chemical combination, although such combinations
be few or even unique. Thus calcium combines
directly, readily, violently with oxygen, and forms
but a single compound, lime, which is almost un-
decomposable; hence calcium is held to have the
greatest chemical affinity for oxygen, far more
than the carbon and hydrogen of organic chemistry;
for calcium seems able to take oxygen with avidity
and ease, and to retain it with extreme tenacity.
And it is therefore argued that the chemical affinity
of calcium for oxygen is great, which, under certain
special circumstances, is true, and that the calcic
affinity for oxygen is intrinsically greater than
that of hydrogen with carbon for oxygen, in organic chemistry, which is not true.   For the violence and greatness of the oxycalcic chemical
attraction and affinity occurs only under peculiar
circumstances, under the pressure of the great
forces of fire and our earth, and the actors in this
action discharge heat so extremely, that they have
difficulty in recovering themselves, or retransforming into free states.   The undecomposability of
lime arises, in a great measure, from our having
for its decomposition no earth-power to help us, as

we had for lime's formation; nay, we have that
power against us. If certain metals unite with
oxygen violently, that is owing to causes in a
measure extraneous to them, and does not depend
on the inherent chemical powers of such metals.
Where are these powers? what are the number of
such metals' compound compared with those of
the organic elements? Truly great chemical
affinity therefore is that existing between the four
organic elements, for in these elements alone are
united all the necessaries of chemical activity;
namely, amount, difference, capacity, conductivity
of heat, and proportionate masses. It is no argument to say that these organic elements do not
readily unite to form organic compounds by the
means usually accessible to chemists, namely, fire
and our earth. That these organic elements have
facilities of combination far greater than others, the
number of their compounds wherever produced amply
proves; and that these compounds are easily decomposed by fire is no proof of their small affinities, but
of the great heat capacity of the organic elements,
which, if it makes, as it is known to do, those elements amenable to the distant sun's moderate heat
action, will *à fortiori* make them amenable to the
action of fire, which, being a sun nearer than natural, will, for limited amount of matter, act more
powerfully than our sun. To say that the organic

elements—parents of innumerable compounds—
have little affinity for each other, simply because
their compounds are destroyed by fire, is paradoxi-
cal. To ascribe the multitude of their combinations
to the intervention of "vital force," seems but to
double the difficulty; for the question then arises,
what is this vital force? the truth being, that
the organic elements require a laboratory of their
own, generally an organised being, to work in, because there these elements have a morphigenic
earth-carbon, and an equable heat-source—our
sun—and thus can act undisturbed by the exces-
sive actions of our earth and of fire.

Combustion may be defined as chemical combining action in which fire appears; that is, in
which heat that was somewhere latent assumes
the visible, thermometric phase. All combustion
heat is sun-heat with more or less removes; there
is no other heat-source for the globe but our sun,
and even volcanic fire may be thereto traced.
Sometimes the combustion heat is seen to come
pretty directly from our sun, as when metals burn
with sun-equilibrised oxygen; sometimes the heat
comes from our sun, but in a more roundabout
manner, through our earth, as when pure carbon
burns; sometimes the heat comes from the sun,
but through fire, as when sulphur sulphurises a
metal.

We will, therefore, consider shortly three characteristic types of combustion : the metallic, the carbonic, the sulphurous. In metallic combustion,
we have metal and oxygen, that, free, are at great
latent-heat disequilibrium with our earth, and cor-
relatedly very unlike our earth's matter, to which
metals, however, have, by their mass and conductivity, and even heat capacity, a special relationship. Metallic combustion is therefore brought
about by the vast earth power urging metal and
oxygen to the assumption of an earth-like form ;
and as oxygen and metal together have heat endowments, that is, mass, conductivity, and heat
capacity, that fit them to yield to our earth force,
there is the violent chemical action between
metal, oxygen, and our earth known as metallic
combustion. The violence of the action is quite
explicable by the pressure in the action of our
colossal earth power. The heat seen in the action
is also reasonably referred to the solidification of
highly gaseous oxygen, and to the diminished
fusibility of the burned metal—the latent heat
present in gaseous oxygen being obtained directly
from our sun, and the latent heat of the metal
being traceable to the fire by which the metal was
reduced from its ore, the heat of the fire being
itself also ultimately traceable to our sun. In
oxymetallic burnings, as before noted, there is a

H

change in the oxygen's and metal's melting points,
indicative of correlated latent-heat loss or disoccupation in both, and also a contraction in their
volumes or shapes; and this contraction leads always to a dilatation in things around the actors,
and ultimately to dilatation of our earth, in which
dilatation the heat given out during the action,
as it seems to disappear, is occupied or rendered
latent. This heat of metallic combustion, therefore,
though it seems to be rapidly dissipated, does not
by any means become extinct; it only becomes
latent in dilating our earth. A portion of the
earth oxygen and metal, in oxymetallic combustion, has given up its heat to the general stock;
or has contracted at the expense of some dilatation
elsewhere. This heat was sun-heat in metal and
oxygen coercing the earth power, and was disoccupied when oxygen and metals yielded to earth
power, and became badly fusible solids; and earth-
equilibrised metals in burning, therefore, may be
considered as negative to our earth, which becomes
positive to them during metallic combustion. The
heat of metallic combustion, therefore, may be viewed
as a spark of positive electricity passing from metal
and oxygen to our earth; and we shall see that it is
so by the study of the galvanic battery. And further, by this idea electro-magnetism becomes greatly
elucidated. When metals oxydise or metalloidise,

there is a latent-heat discharge from and through
them into our earth, and metals are thus thrown
into connection with the earth's sun-got latent heat,
which comes now, therefore, to demand our attention.
The earth cannot possess the same sun-got latent
heat over her whole expanse.   The sun-got latent
heat of the earth cannot be the same at her poles as
at her equator.   Considering the enormous capacity
for heat of water, there must be far more sun-got
latent heat at the equator, where there exists per-
ennially sun-heated water, than at the poles,
where there is everlasting ice.   To map out, therefore, the earth's sun-got latent heat, we must
divide her by her equator into two halves, a north
and a south half.   The north half of the earth
will have a latently cold end or pole near the
north pole, and a latently hot end near the equator.   The south half of the earth will have also a
latently cold end or pole near the south pole, and
a latently hot end near the equator.   Further, the
latently cold end of the earth's north half will
be latently colder than the latently cold end of the
earth's south half, because the land clusters more
towards the north pole than towards the south pole,
and there is much less heat capacity in land than in
ice.   So that the heat contrast between the north
pole and the equator is greater than that between
the south pole and the equator, and the earth's north

pole (magnetic) must be the latently coldest part
of her whole expanse, and to this latently cold
part will all sun-got latent-heat currents, discharging into the earth through the metals, be
by preference directed. Further, there is nothing
to hinder the sun-got latent heat of the earth
from being affected and modified by secular,
annual, diurnal, climateric, local, terric or volcanic, solar or electric causes; on the contrary,
we might reasonably, necessarily expect such dis-
turbances. If such be the distribution of the sun-
got latent heat of the earth, what direction should
a metalloidising metal, discharging sun-got latent
heat into the earth, assume, if free to move, and
placed in favourable inductive circumstances,
such as a wire solenoid connected with an oxidising metal, zinc, in a galvanic battery or a De la
Rive's apparatus? Such a solenoid or its latent-
heat current will avoid the latently hot parts of
the earth—that is, her equator—and will place itself
at right angles to the equator—that is, move away
from the equator as far as it can; will, in fact,
assume a position parallel to the magnetic meri-
dian of the place: and this, though giving a most
rudimentary rough idea of the cause of electro-
magnetism, still may suffice to connect certain
chemical actions with electro-magnetism.

It is somewhat different when carbon burns. Just

as there is a powerful effort in a gaseous element,
such as oxygen, to equilibrise with a solid element
or with solidity representable by our earth, so
there is analogously as urgent a strain on a solid
element, such as carbon, to equilibrise with a
gaseous element or with our sun, and both the
gaseous and the solid elements will thus equilibrise, if they possess the requisite aptitudes of
mass, conductivity, and heat capacity. In free
carbon, therefore, we note great solidity or negativeness seeking violently for the gaseous or positive
latent-heat equilibrium, and having also the powers
of taking this equilibrium. When, therefore,
free solid carbon is presented to gaseous oxygen,
we have to oxygen seeking solidity or earth-equilibrium, an object, carbon, representing perfectly
such an equilibrium. But further, we have also
gaseous oxygen representing to carbon the positiveness it seeks. Hence the two elements rush
violently into mutual equilibrium, and burn into
carbonic anhydrid gas. The carbon assumes a
highly dilated form, and oxygen a more condensed
liquefiable form. Hence part of the heat we see
in this action has come from the contracting
oxygen, but not all the heat; for things around
burning and dilating carbon are forced to contract,
and this contraction furnishes part of the heat of
carbonic combustion. In oxycarbonic combustion,

therefore, a portion of our earth, free carbon,
instead of giving heat to the general store, by
its capacities, conductivity and dilatation, takes
heat thence, and part of the heat seen in the
combustion of carbon comes ultimately from our
earth, which, in order to furnish this heat, contracts. In the combustion of carbon, therefore,
a great part of the heat seen has been, as it were,
squeezed out of the contracting things around, and
thus ultimately for our earth, to which, unlike the
metals in their combustions, carbon is positive.
So that were we viewing the metallic and carbonic combustions from an electric standpoint,
we would say that in the metallic combustion
there was discharged into the actors negative
electricity from the earth, and in the carbonic
combustion positive. Nor would this make much
difference between the heat seen in both cases, for
we know that there is not much visible difference
between a positive and negative electric spark
from an electric-machine. The heat abstracted
thus by burning carbon from the general store
and our earth is also not annihilated, but is slowly
restored to our earth by the action of plant life
on carbonic anhydrid gas. But· even this heat,
apparent in carbonic combustion, is still nothing
but sun-heat returning to us again after many
removes and transmigrations.

In combustions such as the oxysulphurous, the action is restricted to the actors, and the heat passes from unliquefied free oxygen, which becomes by its sulphurous combustion almost liquefiable, to solid sulphur, which is raised to a gas; so that this action is simple, and from the general heat stock no heat is withdrawn or added.

CHAPTER IX.

Chemical decomposition. Relation of chemicals to each other, as ingredients of compounds, is not that of attraction, but of latent-heat balance or equilibrium. The decomposition of the red oxide of mercury by heat is the analogue in chemical action of electric repulsion. Causes of the stability of compounds. Spontaneous explosive decomposition: various decompositions and decomposing actions and means.

In studying chemical decomposition, we begin, not with two chemicals that are free, but that are compounded; not with two chemicals having different latent heats, but the same latent heats; not with heat disequilibrium, but with equilibrium of actors; and in decomposition we end by disequilibrising, as in composition we finished with equilibrising, the actors; in short, chemical decomposition is the converse of combination. The first step, therefore, in the study of chemical decomposition consists in the clear understanding of the relations of the ingredients of compounds to each other. Let us consider a metallic protoxide such as water. To combine and produce water, free oxygen and hydrogen attracted each other and the earth, because there was between the three mutual latent-heat

difference. This difference having been by combination equilibrised, the oxygen and hydrogen are
heat-balanced, and cease to attract each other; for
if you hold, as is done in chemistry, that attraction
of the actors solely caused chemical combining
action, and that that attraction thereafter persists,
the action should not stop at combination, but get
thereafter stronger and stronger. But such is
never the case. In chemical combining action,
we see an intense activity followed by as profound
a calm; and since action thus stops, its causes
must have ceased also, as they do by the neutralisation of the forces of the action's causation,
by the equilibration of the latent heats of the combiners, and often of those of their surroundings.
Again, if the ingredients of compounds attracted
each other forcibly, they would approach, and
there would be changes in the physical properties
of compounds even after combination; and as we
do not see such changes, ingredients of compounds
cannot attract each other. So that the truer idea
of the relation of the ingredients of compounds
to each other is, not that they are attracting, but
that one exists beside the other, either solidified
or melted, or vaporised into a latent-heat equilibrium with each other, and, besides, often also
with our sun, or earth, or fire; in which equilibrium the ingredients have equal or like latent

heats. It is, therefore, not attraction that keeps
the ingredients of a compound together, but their
relations of balance to the latent heat of things
around and of themselves. The two ingredients
of water, oxygen and hydrogen, although they
do not attract, cannot separate; because to separate they must become gases, and being in water
liquids, to gasify they need heat, which under
common circumstances they cannot obtain; they
therefore remain side by side indefinitely, having
a position with reference to our earth's latent
heat. The earth has a sun-got latent-heat
polarity; for she has her latently cold or negative
pole at the magnetic pole, and a latently hot
positive pole at her magnetic equator. To this terrestrial sun-got latent-heat polarity the latent heat
of the ingredients of water is related. Oxygen's
latent heat, as an ingredient of water, is still
latently heat-positive to the earth, seeing that
oxygen is in water fluid, but can in lime become
infusibly solid. Hydrogen in water, however, is
as like or heat-similar to the earth as it can be;
so that a molecule of water has a latent-heat
polarity to the earth, like a swung magnet, the
latently hot oxygen turning to the latently cold
pole of the earth, and the latently cold hydrogen
to the latently hot equator.

But sun-got latent heat can be shown by the

study of the galvanic battery to be electricity,
therefore the ingredients of compounds have
similar, or at least electricities in equilibria or
neutralised. So that in simple direct combination
we start with non-equilibrium, or with a latent
heat or electric difference in the combining, and
thus with attraction between them. In simple
decomposition we commence with the reverse, with
equilibrium in ingredients with a latent heat or
electric similarity in them and non-attraction, and
even with a possibility of repulsion; for as chemical action is electric, there exists in some of these
actions repulsion, as in others attraction. Repulsion is as characteristic a force of electricity as
attraction. Attraction is a highly essential force
for combination; but on combination everything
is changed. The combiners differ from the same
when combined *in toto*, in latent heat, and thus,
in form and electricities; no chemical property is
the same in the two; and not even attraction remains, for the cause of attraction—the difference
of latent heat or electricities—has even been reversed, and now gives rise to a possibility of repulsion between ingredients.

Oxygen and mercury (in the red oxide of mercury) have like latent heats. While uniting, the
two had unlike, and united, they have like latent
heats. But latent heat may be proved galvanic

electricity, so that combining mercury and oxygen
have unlike or opposite electricities, and attract
each other; and compounded oxygen and mercury
have the same or electricities in equilibrium, and
therefore, far from attracting, *tend* rather to repel
each other.   It is, in fact, this similarity of electricities in the ingredients of compounds that
makes their separation by heat alone possible; for
how could mercury and oxygen in their oxide
separate from each other, as we know they do, by
heat alone, without repelling each other?   As
simple union involves the idea of attraction in
the uniting, so simple and uncomplicated decomposition, or separation by heat alone, presupposes
a repulsion among the decomposing ingredients;
hence repulsion comes to play a part, at least, in
simple chemical decomposing action.   Oxygen and
mercury, in their oxide, have similar electricities,
and are thus charged with that force which we
know produces repulsion. If you further heat them,
you charge them, for a time, more and more with
this force latent heat, and their repulsion becomes
stronger and stronger, and passes eventually into
separation.   But by heating you not only increase
repulsion, you do more; you give also the possibility to the compounded ingredients of retrans-
formation; and this explains why you are enabled
by heat alone to decompose certain metallic oxides.

Your heating tends always to arouse more or less repulsion of ingredients for each other; but this repulsion is not alone sufficient for decomposition, just as we saw that attraction was not alone enough for combination. For decomposition, retransforming-heat discharges are also necessary; for decomposition is inversely analogous to composition. If your heat is not enough for the purpose of retransforming the decomposing, or even if they have a difficulty in receiving heat, it is in vain that the heat is offered, and that it always originates the repulsion. In direct, simple, chemical decomposition there must happen the reverse of chemical combination — namely, induction, repulsion, latent-heat changes, retransformations, and, finally, freedom and non-equilibrium. The stability of chemical compounds depends on the nature of their latent-heat equilibria; and there are three principal equilibria in chemistry—the inorganic, the organic, and the minor. Of these three, the inorganic or terrestrial equilibrium tends to produce some of the stablest compounds—stability meaning difficulty of decomposition; for our earth, being large, passive, and latently cold, has the power of impressing this latent coldness or negativeness on compounds at equilibrium with her, and such compounds lack, therefore, heat, one of the causes of chemical changeableness or spontaneous activity. As conductivity is necessary to obtain in chemical action equilibrium with our earth, metals often occur in earth-equilibrised compounds. Non-oxidisable or noble metals have large equivalents and weights, and thus very small heat capacities or capability of taking sun-latent heat or forms, and these metals are even free like the earth, and are thus, when free, at their best equilibrium; hence these metals do not oxidise readily, and when oxidised easily regain the fredom most congenial to their heat constitution, or, as it is said, the oxides of noble metals are easily reduced. The oxidisable metals, such as calcium, have small equivalents and weights, and are thus heat capacious, and able to take latent heat from furnaces, and also to give it away earthwards, and when free are not like the earth, and thus not at their best equilibrium. Such metals, combining with oxygen, undergo the whole of our earth's powerful influence; and oxygen and calcium are at combination exhaustively drained by our earth of their latent heat, and become from fusible solid and unliquefied gas, reduced in lime to solid infusibility. Hence such oxides as lime are difficult to decompose; their ingredients were urged into combination by a force—our earth—which we cannot, in our efforts at their separation, command or imitate. Such

oxides as lime are very latently cold compounds,
and their ingredients have little of that force that
can produce spontaneous decomposition or change;
and if we try artificially to decompose lime, we
find a difficulty to give back to its ingredients,
oxygen and calcium, the heat they in combining
lost to our earth. To retransform into metallic
free fusible calcium and into gaseous oxygen, the
solid oxygen and infusible calcium, ingredients of
oxide of calcium, must obtain back the latent
heat they disoccupied at their combination and
persolidification, and this heat is, from its amount,
difficult for us to give and for the ingredients to
accept, seeing that they are urged by no great
force to receive this heat for their decomposition,
as they were when free by our earth to discharge
heat for combination. For the combination of
calcium and oxygen we had our earth force for
us; for the decomposition of the combination of
oxygen and calcium we have no such force in our
favour, but rather against us. Hence the oxide
of calcium and its congeners are much more easily
made than unmade. Lime does not decompose of
its own accord, nor can you readily decompose it
by heat alone. If you define stability in compounds as difficulty of decomposition, then combinations having organic or carbon equilibrium must
always be less stable than those having good ter-

restrial equilibrium; for, as a centre of heat equi-
poise, carbon is an equilibrium in equilibrio, and
lesser carbon belongs to the greater earth; and
thus the heat equilibration furnished by conductive
carbon is a subject one, controlled by our earth.
Further, the very power that makes carbon a great
organic element—that is, the power of taking heat
from a distant sun—*à fortiori* makes carbon still
more amenable to fire, or a sun nearer and stronger
than natural; that is, carbon's heat constitution
makes it readily obey either fire, or our sun, or
our earth, if any of the three preponderate. As
long as the usual natural sun and earth equilibrium is retained around carbon-equilibrised compounds—that is, organic compounds—they are
stable enough, and will often last for ages. But
suppose we alter the relative situations of earth
and sun to carbon-equilibrised chemical compounds, which may be readily done by bringing
fire on them in the presence or absence of oxygen
or positive bodies: in contact with fire, or a sun
nearer than natural, and oxygen, carbon, light,
heat capacious, conductive, takes heat readily, and
sun forms, as carbonic oxide and anhydrid: in
contact with fire, and nothing else but our earth,
carbon, light, heat capacious, and conductive, gives
then its heat to our earth, and always appears as
charcoal.

Again, carbon's great latent coldness makes it a
powerful demander of heat, and carbon's lightness
and heat capacity make it retain the heat demanded by morphigenesis or transformation latent
in it, and thus carbon takes and retains so much
heat that it is only the most heat-capacious and
latently hottest of the elements, nitrogen, oxygen,
hydrogen, that can act with it. Again, in organic
actions during life, the sun takes a preponderating
share; in animals by respired oxygen, which is a
sun element *par excellence;* in plants by sunlight
and respired carbonic anhydrid, in which carbon
has become a sun element by oxygenic combination; hence it follows that organic compounds are
of a latently or even of a thermometrically hotter
type than the inorganic, and have thus that force
heat which gives chemical activity. At death, animal and plant respiration stops, and the direct
sun action thus ceases, and the chemical elements
that existed in animal and plant are now in the
dead subjected solely to the common or inorganic
terro-solar equilibrium, and have to adapt themselves thereto, and become thus minerals; for
these elements are the most heat-plastic known,
and the heat constitution of matter exists as well
for heat as for cold, as well for our sun as for our
earth, as well for the positive as for the negative
force of nature. The minor equilibria of chemistry

I

are those which chemicals furnish to each other,
and among such we naturally meet with the most
unstable compounds. Nitrogen forms with oxygen,
chlorine, bromine, &c., compounds one characteristic of which is their often spontaneous, violent,
explosive decomposibility ; and this is intelligible
if we take into account the heat constitution of
nitrogen, and the equilibria that oxygen, chlorine,
&c., can give it in combination. Nitrogen, we
have often had occasion to state, is nearly the
latently hottest of free terrestrial matter, and most
prone to take a solar equilibrium ; for nitrogen
exists as four-fifths of the atmosphere, and thus for
nitrogen the sun has the most affection ; and as
such things, at least in chemistry, are reciprocal,
nitrogen has also a like sun attraction.   When
nitrogen leaves a solar for a terrestrial, or, what is
as good, a carbonic equilibrium, as it does when
nitrogen becomes part of ammonia or part of
cyanogen and other organic compounds, it is clear
that nitrogen is less likely to form unstable or explosive compounds ; for nitrogen has in our earth
and very latently cold carbon the most anti-solar
or strongest equilibrium, for our earth and carbon
best resist nitrogen's tendency to go sunwards.
But when nitrogen is in combination solely with
oxygen or chlorine, &c., it is bound to solar elements that, far from preventing nitrogen's ten-

dency sunwards, tend that way themselves, and
consequently explosive and easy decomposition of
such nitrogenous compounds arises. All equilibria,
however, from the fact that they are equilibria, are
stable if left in perfectly congenial heat surroundings, and thus undisturbed by extraneous heat
agencies; but this is impossible, in the present
state of things, to many compounds that seem
therefore to undergo spontaneous decomposition;
and most compounds are further decomposable by
art, for, obliged by the necessities of existence, or
urged by curiosity, we have gradually empirically
found out many means of destroying the equilibria of the ingredients of compounds, in which
processes the use of fire or of a sun nearer and
more powerful than the natural sun is greatly employed.

The means of chemical decomposition are—1st,
Inherent latent heat ; 2d, Extraneous heat alone,
in the galvanic, electric, or other phases ; 3d,
Extraneous heat together with other chemicals ;
4th, Presence of other chemicals without extraneous heat.   And simple direct chemical decompositions or separations consist in—1st, Inductions;
2d, Repulsions ; 3d, Heat changes ; 4th, Retrans-
formation; 5th, Non-equilibrium or freedom.

That heat alone should frequently cause chemical
decomposition is what was to be expected, and

that heat does not do so more frequently is what is more difficult to explain.

Electricity, as a means of chemical decomposition, acts as a more intense and inducting phase of heat, and is a powerful agent; and the electric spark is known to decompose compounds refractory to the fire-got phase of energy. For an electric spark, whether negative or positive, may be considered as passing from one portion of our earth to another, and the spark is thus able to give or take earthwards heat from ingredients of compounds undergoing its decomposing action; for the spark has heat in itself, and can also open up a passage for heat earthwards if such be necessary, and the spark can probably by inductions increase the repulsion to which ingredients of compounds are prone.

The action of the galvanic battery on chemical decomposition will be studied when we treat of galvanism.

A compound, say water, may be decomposed by the mere contact of a metal such as potassium; for the two ingredients of water, oxygen and hydrogen, exist in water side by side, like two touching billiard-balls, not attracting, but in equilibrium, free to revolve round each other, but in water retaining a definite position because of the relations of the latent-heat states of water's oxygen and hydrogen to the latent-heat state of the earth. The oxygenic ball, being latently hot or positive, will be related to the earth's latently cold negative or arctic or antarctic pole, and the hydrogen being latently cold and negative, will be related to the earth's latently hot or positive equator. In fact, the earth is a very large sun-got latent-heat magnet, and the molecule of water, composed of one oxygenic ball and another of hydrogen, is a very small latent-heat magnet earth-swung. As the two ingredients of water, the oxygenic and hydrogenic balls, are not attracting, but in equilibrio, they can move round each other, or indeed away from each other ; and the two balls will shift their positions if you place, instead of the earth, another latent-heat magnet, as is the platinum and zinc plates connected by the wire in a galvanic battery, and the balls will then take positions not in reference to the earth, but to the nearer and latently cold or negative zinc, and the latently hot or positive platinum plates. And the two balls will move away from each other if you decompose water. When the two balls, the ingredients of water, oxygen and hydrogen, change, in the galvanic battery, their polarity, no change is seen to occur in them in the water, because to change aspect and state or form, not change of polarity, but of their latent heats, is needed by them. If you bring potassium

upon the oxygen and hydrogen of water, you produce results analogous to those that a third billiard-
ball, a potassic one, not in equilibrium, but in
motion towards it, would occasion, by striking the
water's oxygenic ball opposite the hydrogenic one.
The equilibrising potassic ball would, on striking
the water's oxygenic ball, remain beside it, balanced
or stopped, and the potassic motion would be
transmitted to the hydrogenic ball opposite, which,
quite free to move, would at once pass away from
the oxygenic ball. There is energy, force *vive*,
potential in potassium and oxygen, for they are
earth-disequilibrised and moving into earth or the
solid equilibrium, and this force is spent in disequilibrising hydrogen, which moves up into the
solar equilibrium. It is always so : on one side
we have one set of phenomena, balanced on the
other side by their opposites.

On the one hand we have solidification, contraction, diminished motion, latent cold, negativeness, or terrestrial phenomena.   On the other
hand, on the opposite side, in polar, correlated
relations, we have gasification, dilatation, increased
motion, latent heat, positiveness, or solar phenomena.   The sun and earth typically represent
these great natural forces.   When free carbon
decomposes metallic oxides, it never does so by its
unaided powers, as potassium does water, but heat

is always also employed. At high temperatures the ingredients of a metallic oxide — namely, oxygen and metal, have of themselves a tendency to take sun-equilibrised shapes, and if we add carbon we increase this tendency greatly, and decomposition or reduction occurs.

Free hydrogen will take, under certain circumstances, the oxygen from the oxide of iron, for free hydrogen has the position of advantage over the iron in the oxide, inasmuch as free hydrogen has a tendency towards taking equilibrium, has potential energy, force *vive*, while the iron of the oxide has equilibrium and less force *vive*; and in the decomposition of the oxide of iron by hydrogen it becomes water, and takes the iron's oxide or earth shape, and hydrogen then gives to the oxide iron its (hydrogen's) free shape; and free solar potentialised iron will do the same by oxidised or equilibrised hydrogen, and will decompose water.

CHAPTER X.

Nature of bases : the earth and carbon, connection of their ingredients.   Nature of acids : oxyacids : hydracids : acido-basic
combinations : salts.   ˈ

Two elements combine chemically into one compound, because when single the two elements were
at latent-heat dissimilarity or disequilibrium, and
thus require equilibrium; and after chemical
attraction, contact, and latent-heat discharge, they
do always, as long as compounded, get latent-heat
similarity or equilibrium with respect to the two
themselves.   But in chemistry there exists other
equilibria beside the special one of the ingredients
of compounds to themselves ; as, for example, the
general equilibrium of earth and sun, of which no
chemical is independent; and in this last equilibrium alone chemicals find repose ; that is, it is
only when they reach this last equilibrium haven,
as happens in salts, that they are greatly freed from
the restless, stormy, combining, or equilibrium-
seeking activity, and rest a little from their
chemical labours.   From certain peculiarities of
chemical actions, this *juste milieu* of sun, earth,

and chemical or the equo-terro-solar equilibrium
is not in every inter-elementary combination at
one step attained. When what has been called
bases, that is, metallic protometalloidids, arise,
a latently hot metalloid, a latently cold object,
chiefly our earth or carbon, and a suitable metal
heat-transmitter together act. Hence the metallically facilitated heat discharges from all the hot
actors pass readily into our large, passive, latently
cold, heat-attracting earth, or into infusible carbon, and the earth's or carbon's latent coldness,
negativeness, is in the compound mean largely
assumed, and these resulting metallic protometalloidids come to represent our earth in miniature, or carbon, and are negative ; that is, with
reference to the general equilibrium of our sun
and earth, these mineral metallic protometalloidids, the bases, have too much of our earth, are
too negative, to suit the presence of the other
great chemical force, our sun and its representatives ; so that although the ingredients of
these metallic protometalloid bases are at perfect
latent-heat equilibrium with each other, the bases
themselves have too much of our earth, are too
negative, and are not at equilibrium with certain
chemicals, in which there is too much of our
sun to harmonise with the existence of our earth,
as happens, as we shall presently see, in what are

called radicles of acids. The characteristic of a
base therefore is that, in its latent-heat mean of
combination, the form or latent heat of a latently
cold object preponderatingly enters, and this latently
cold object is our earth, and often, for organic
chemistry, carbon, or sometimes, though, for obvious reasons, more seldom and imperfectly, even
latently cold platinum, as in the interesting
chemicals called Reiset's bases. A metal, connected always with the latently cold object, essentially preponderates in a base, as latently hot
metalloid, or very latently hot hydrogen, acting
as such, prevail in the acid's radicles. In fact,
upon the metal chiefly depends the power of the
ingredients of a base to take on the basic latent
heat or earth or carbon, or, in short, the negative
form; and this metal ingredient of the base becomes thus an indication, and even measure, of
this direct earth or carbon, or negative connection
of the base, as we see more easily in organic
chemistry, where carbon, the latently cold object,
is always analytically demonstrable, and is found
to increase or decrease in exact ratio with the rise
or fall of the base's metal, which in organic
chemistry is chiefly hydrogen. Hence we have
a right to conclude, by strict analogy, that inorganic ammonia (NH_3), having three volumes or
equivalents of metal, hydrogen has more of our

earth than water (HO) has, which has one
equivalent of the metal hydrogen ; and if our earth
were like carbon, this would be demonstrable by
actual analysis in inorganic ammonia (NH_3E_{3x});
for we find, in the organic ammonias, each equivalent of hydrogen of inorganic ammonia can be
substituted by radicles, having each its own
amount of carbon, as in triethylamine (C_4H_5)
(C_4H_5) (C_4H_5) (N), the organic ammonia, compared
with (E_xH) (E_xH) (E_xH) (N) ammonia of mineral
chemistry. The essential of a base, we repeat,
is the preponderance in it, by direct connection,
of a latently cold negative object, chiefly our
earth or carbon. The typical form of a mineral
base is solid and insoluble, for such also is the
average form of our earth, which the base in
miniature represents. But just as the form of the
earth itself varies from its medium form of solidity to its atmospheric, unliquefiable gaseity, so
the form of the base has limits of variation, keeping short of extreme unliquefiable gaseity, and
tending always far more to solidity, infusibility,
insolubility ; and so mineral bases are solids or
somewhat *near* it; for even ammonia is, for a
gas, very easy to solidify, compared say with
hydrochloric acid, &c.

A base being a direct compound of metalloid,
metal and our earth will be a latent-heat mean

of the three, struck according to the amount of
latent heat, the specific heats and weights, &c., of
the three; hence the base ammonia, though having
a basic portion of the earth, because produced by
latently hot hydrogen and by nitrogen, which
last is hotter and about half as heat capacious as
oxygen, is not as latently cold in form as are the
bases produced by oxygen with the other metals.
To form what is called a base, a certain amount
of latent coldness or negativeness is needful;
hence the metalloidal ingredient of a base, which
we know to be the latently hot ingredient, is reduced always to a minimum in bases, and you
cannot augment it without the certainty of destroying basic character in a base so treated. The
other component of the base is a metal, and the
metal we know is of itself already rather negative, and in forming the base this metal becomes
still more negative by virtual contact with our
latently cold earth or carbon: if the metal forming the base is positive, such as hydrogen, and
further connected with a very positive metalloid,
such as nitrogen, then the necessary basic negativeness is obtained by increasing the amount of
hydrogen, and thus taking the latently cold object,
the earth or carbon, largely into partnership in
the combination, as we see in ammonia (NH_3E_{3x})
and certain organic bases.

Several kinds of bases exist: the most interesting are the oxy bases, the nitro base ammonia,
the organic bases, the sulpho bases. In all these
bases there is the characteristic preponderance of
the metallic with our earth or carbon over the
metalloid ingredient. All the ingredients of mineral bases disoccupy heat in becoming basic—that
means, pass from solar to terric forms, and become thus negative. In all inorganic bases, since
our earth virtually enters into their mean of combination, she may be considered to have chemically
moved a step in the direction of the oxygen in
the oxy bases, of the nitrogen in the nitro bases,
and of sulphur in the sulpho bases; and in the
corresponding hydra, oxy, and sulpho acids, the
hydrogen, oxygen, and sulphur have descended a
convergent chemical step towards our earth, to
meet the bases, so to speak; hence the reason that
oxy, nitro, sulpho bases best suit the oxy, hydra,
and sulpho acids. In oxy bases and the nitro
base ammonia, our earth has a morphic part;
and in the organic bases, carbon is morphically
and bodily present. Between carbon and the
other ingredients of an organic base—hydrogen,
nitrogen, and oxygen—there is not only attraction, but combination, for such is possible and
inevitable. Between our earth and the other ingredients of oxy bases, and of the nitro base

ammonia, there cannot be actual combination, but
there is a something to indicate their intimate
relations : there is the first step towards chemical
combination, the attraction. This attraction of
relation to the earth of metals and metalloids,
assuming by combination earth-equilibrium and
basicness, has been called electro-magnetism; and
we come to see it best in the phenomena of the
galvanic battery. As the ingredients of certain
organic compounds have a constant relation,
attraction, polarity to carbon, so the ingredients
of inorganic protoxides or bases, or hydrated acids,
&c., have a relation, attraction, polarity to the
earth, best seen in liquids or in water. The ingredients of water are oxygen and hydrogen; of
these two ingredients, hydrogen, when free, will
tend to act the negative or latently cold part; for
hydrogen, from its metallicity, can become, from
heat conduction, readily cold, being always, so to
speak, in the presence and in relation with our
vast latently cold earth, so that free hydrogen is
always negative to free oxygen. As a component
of water, hydrogen is no longer latently negative
to oxygen; the two have similar neutralised or
balanced latent heats, but the two ingredients of
water, oxygen and hydrogen, differ as to their
latent-heat relations to our earth. Hydrogen, as
a constituent of water, is as latently cold, or as

like our earth, as hydrogen can ever be as a protoxide, and is thus earth-negative compared with
oxygen, which we know can become, as an oxide,
as in solid infusible lime, much latently colder,
much liker our solid earth, than oxygen is in
liquid water; and oxygen is thus, while in water,
still latently hot or positive to the earth. So that,
of the two ingredients of water, hydrogen is negative and oxygen positive to our earth's latent
heat; and the two are therefore not mixed up
confusedly in water, but are arranged with an
earth polarity, as the plus and minus marks in
an inductively electrified object, or in a steel-bar
magnet, as may be diagrammatically represented
in the following manner:—

+ –	+ –	+ –	+ –	+ –
O I	O I	O I	O I	O I
+ –	+ –	+ –	+ –	+ –
O I	O I	O I	O I	O I

So that if we conceive the whole of the water of
the northern hemisphere to be one molecule of
water, that molecule would act as an earth-swung
magnet, the hydrogen being the latently cold or
negative pole, pointing to the latently hot or
positive earth's equator, and the oxygen being the
latently hot or positive pole, pointing to the latently
cold earth's north pole. In the organic bases no
such earth polarity exists, because these bases are

not connected with the earth, but with carbon; for
it is this freedom from earth interference and
polarity, possibly by the employment of carbon,
that gives the peculiar special character and aspect
to organic chemistry. Such are the relations to
our earth of the metallic protometalloidids, and
even, as we shall presently see, of hydrated acids,
particularly if they be fluid or in fusion—that is,
if their ingredients be free to move; and it must
be recollected that we cannot distinguish this
checkered polar arrangement of the hydrogen and
oxygen of water, or of any fluid protometalloidid,
by the optical sense, because both oxygen and
hydrogen are molecular, and further, have in water
equal or like latent heats, that is, equal or like
forms and characters. Further, oxygen and hydrogen have in water this polar position to the
earth, because she is herself a great sun-got
latent-heat magnet, that is, has a sun-got latently
hot equator and a latently cold pole. If, therefore, we present to the oxygen and hydrogen of
water, instead of the earth, another and nearer
magnet, as we shall find is the latently hot or
positive platinum and latently cold positive zinc
plates, and the connecting wire of a galvanic
battery, then the magnetically earth-swung ingredients of water, oxygen and hydrogen, will
leave their magnetic earth position, and will at

once oscillate into a magnetic direction in relation
to the nearer galvanic magnet-of zinc, platinum,
and wire; for we have tried to prove that oxygen
and hydrogen, as ingredients of fluid water, are
not attracting, but in equilibrium, and free to move
round each other, and in so moving, they do not
decompose, for, to do that, they must retransform
into gases, and, so to do, they must obtain heat,
and this their mere oscillating movement round
each other cannot give them; nor when so moving
do we readily distinguish, even with the microscope, the particles of oxygen and hydrogen from
each other, for the two are very molecular, and
have in water like forms correlatively given them
by their similarity of latent heat.

We repeat, the characteristic of bases is, that
they are much latently colder or more negative
than all their free ingredients, and this is brought
about by a free and large connection with a
latently cold object, chiefly our earth or carbon;
and this important negative connection is generally
established by a metal. Now metals are themselves already somewhat negative, so that in a
base there exists two negative ingredients, the
metal and our earth or carbon. But there exists a
remarkable metal, hydrogen, which, far from being
intrinsically negative, is, on the contrary, intrinsically positive, and only acts negatively because

K

from its conductivity and heat capacity it readily
loses heat in any direction, and becomes as cold
during action as the coldest actor that predominates near it, generally our earth or carbon. Being
intrinsically positive, hydrogen, therefore, to form
a base, must take our latently cold earth into
partnership much more largely than the common
or more negative metals need do—that is, it
requires more equivalents of positive but earth-
connected hydrogen to form a base than it does
of the common or more negative metals; for the
more the hydrogen is used in such compounds, the
more the earth or carbon is reciprocally, correlatively used. Hence water (HO), that has but one
equivalent of hydrogen, and thus only one of
earth, is not a base, but ammonia (NH_3), that has
three equivalents of hydrogen or of the corresponding earth or carbon, is basic. Hydrogen with
oxygen does not form a proper base at all, but
that most remarkable chemical water. Water is
a metallic protoxide, formed of one equivalent of
a latently hot metalloid, oxygen, and only one of
a metalloidal metal, hydrogen. Hence water
never loses its metalloidal nature quite completely,
and yet water has also very stable earth connection; and, from its form in nature, we also see
this double relation of water to earth and sun,
to matter and to life, for water's shape in nature

is liquid, or the medium between gaseity and solidity; so that water has a central position in chemistry that few chemicals enjoy. Water's chief predominant characteristic is, therefore, neutrality, centrality; and in this central position water is on the confines of acidity, basity (?), salinity (?). In some circumstances, therefore, water can act the metalloidal or acid part, though much less perfectly than if water were more decidedly metalloidal; and water can appear somewhat as an acid, and hence it may dissolve acids, as the hydrochloric, without injuring their acidity. Sometimes water acts the part of a base, always worse than a proper base—that is, water gives the terric equilibrium to the hydrated acids; and water also dissolves bases without destroying their basic nature, and sometimes water enters freely into the saline compounds, as what is called water of crystallisation. We repeat, that the metal hydrogen, since it is the hottest known, to form a base which is a negative body, must be assisted greatly by our latently cold earth or carbon, and consequently a number of equivalents of hydrogen are used, which necessitate a corresponding amount of earth or carbon, as in ammonia $(\overline{N, HE_xHE_xHE_x})$ or triethylamine $(\ddot{N}H_4\overline{C_5H_4C_5}$ $\overline{H_4C_5})$; and the base ammonia is alkaline, or comes to resemble naturally the bases that the

latently hottest of the common metals, potassium
and sodium, &c., form.

Acids are the opposite in heat nature to bases.
In acids it is positiveness or metalloidal elements
that preponderate; in acids, therefore, there is too
much of our sun still present to suit the existence
of our earth, or for just terro-solar equilibrium.
There are two kinds of acids, called the oxyacids
and the hydracids.

Let us first examine a typical oxyacid, the
sulphuric. Sulphuric acid is composed of its
anhydrid (SO_3) and water (HO), and when the
anhydrid (SO_3) is united to the water, there is
reason to hold that the oxygen of the water passes
to the anhydrid (SO_3), and makes the acid's radicle (SO_4O), to which the hydrogen is united to
make the complete or hydrated sulphuric acid—
thus, SO_4O radicle, H metal; so that sulphuric
acid is not so much the compound of water (HO)
and the anhydrid (SO_3) as of the radicle (SO_4O)
and hydrogen (SO_4O)H). This is best seen in
certain electrolyses, and is caused by the law of
duality of chemical combination, itself produced
by the existence in chemistry of positive and negative, of the latently hot and cold, of the two great
chemical forces, sun and earth; so that in sulphuric acid all the hot elements, sulphur and the
four equivalents of oxygen, come to be grouped

together on one pole, as what is called the radicle
(SO_8O), and hydrogen occupies the negative or
earth cold pole of the compound, the sulphuric
acid (SO_8O+H); so that in sulphuric acid and
in oxyacids generally we have three things to
study—the oxyanhydrids (SO_3), the oxyacid radicles (SO_3O), and the complete or proper or hydrated
acid ($SO_8O)H$). Whether we examine sulphuric
acid as it exists in the proper or hydrated condition ($SO_8O)H$), or in its radicle (SO_8O), or in
its anhydrid (SO_3), we at once see that the metalloidal elements there prevail. In the anhydrid
(SO_8), in the radicle (SO_3O), nothing but metalloidal elements exist—viz., sulphur and oxygen,
and in the hydrated acid ($SO_3O)H$) a metal, hydrogen, and thus an earth connection does certainly
exist. But this metal is hydrogen, the most metalloidal known, and it is the hydrogen of water
with the smallest earth connection possible; so
that sulphuric acid and oxyacids may be defined
as a group of various metalloids (SO_3O), (NO_6O),
united to our earth by the most metalloidal of
metallic links, hydrogen. However, in the hydrated oxyacid there is for the metalloids this
important earth link, hydrogen; hence in hydrated
oxyacids there is our earth to balance the metalloids of the acid, and in these acids there is therefore an element of stability. If we regard the

isolated oxyanhyrid (SO_3), however, and still more
the oxyacid radicles (SO_3O), we find as a rule no
proper element of good stability in them, for the
ingredients of oxyanhydrids and oxyacid radicles
are all sun elements, latently hot metalloids, sometimes massed together in groups of large numbers,
as in the chlorine oxyacids, and they therefore cannot heat-balance each other at all, or do so with
difficulty and extreme instability. A number of
the oxyanhydrids, therefore, cannot be obtained at
all; some are produced with difficulty, many are
unstable when obtained; and if some there be that
are, as the carbonic, phosphoric, sulphurous anhydrids, easily produced and stable, it is because
carbon and phosphorus are latently cold enough
metalloids to balance the oxygen of their acid anhydrids; and so is sulphur, seeing that in sulphurous
anhydrid it has only to balance two equivalents
of oxygen. But this remarkable instability of
oxyanhydrids, even the most pronounced, dis-
appears at once when the anhydrids get water or
a base with which to combine, that is, when they
obtain, instead of their own minor and weak equilibrium, the strong one of our earth. If, therefore,
the anhydrids of oxyacids be generally of difficult
isolation and unstable, their radicles are *à fortiori*
still more and always so, for the cause of anhydrid instability is still more decided in the oxyacid

radicles than in the oxyanhydrids, since more
metalloids exist in radicles than in anhydrids ;
and it is only the strong earth-equilibrium given
by hydrogen of water to the radicle that makes
its existence in the oxyacid possible.   A hydrated
oxyacid is therefore a chemical in which the
negative ingredient, represented by a metal, is
reduced to a minimum ; and not only so, but the
metal is hydrogen of water, by far the least
negative of all the metals, and having the least
possible earth connection, for it is the hydrogen of
water ; and while the negative metallic ingredient
is in hydrated oxyacids reduced to a minimum, in
very unnegative hydrogen, the positive or metalloidal ingredients are generally in large groups
and masses, or greatly preponderate.   Hence we
conclude that oxyacids are positive, metalloidal,
solar chemicals, having, like elementary and single
metalloids, the solar form and position of constraint or advantage over our earth, and tending
strongly to collapse into equilibrium with our
earth's latent heat or form, that is, to pass into
denser forms.   If it were not for hydrogen, no
oxyacid would be possible, for the hydrogen of
water is what gives to the anhydrids of oxyacids a
stable terrestrial equilibrium, a latent-heat mean
of combination of such a heat nature, from the positiveness of hydrogen, as to be not a saline mean,

but an acid one. But it is also true that, without
such chemicals as the metalloidal oxyanhydrids,
hydrogen of water could not strike the acid mean
of combination. The oxyanhydrids are very unlike the bases; several of the former are gaseous,
and those that are solids have nevertheless a
solidity very unlike the basic one. The oxyanhydrids are fusible, or volatile, or gaseous, or
soluble, that is, these chemicals have solar
forms, and have occupied, sun-got, latent heat, and
are at disequilibrium with the usual earth form,
and have not enough of earth connection or equilibrium; hence these chemicals take with extreme
avidity an earth equilibrium, and this, generally,
first with water, since water has an earth equilibrium to give, and is a most accessible part of
the earth, is fluid and very heat capacious, and extensively and permeatively present as vapour, &c.
But though water is the easiest and most accessible terrestrial equilibrium for the oxyanhydrids,
yet water is not the best, for water is too positive
and too metalloidal to produce with an oxyanhydrid the just terro-solar equilibrium; this is
alone given by the more negative bases, and particularly the oxybases. For a hydrated oxyacid
there exists an earth link, hydrogen, and an earth
polarity, as exists for a metallic protoxide. Indeed, a metallic protoxide is analogous to a

hydrated oxyacid, only instead of a single equivalent of a metalloid, oxygen of the protoxide
(OME_x), we have a group of metalloids (SO_3O),
called the radicle, for hydrated oxyacids, and hydrogen for their metal, and both the one metalloid,
oxygen of the protoxide, and the group of metalloids of the oxyacid radicles, tend strongly to an
earth equilibrium, which has been attained by the
oxygen of the metallic protoxide through the
metal, and by the acid radicle through the hydrogen. The radicle (SO_3O), therefore, is the positive ingredient or pole of the sulphuric acid, and
will point to where the oxygen of a fluid protoxide
pointed, that is, to the earth's north pole or to
the zinc plate of a galvanic battery ; and indeed
it is chiefly during certain electrolyses that we
see this radicle distinctly present and acting, as
first observed by Miller ; and the hydrogen of the
acid will be its negative pole, and will point to
the earth's equator, or the platinum or copper or
carbon of a galvanic battery, as seen in diagram :—

SO_3O	H	SO_3O	H
+	–	+	–

The acid's radicle magnetically behaves to the
acid's hydrogen and to the earth, just as water's
oxygen to water's hydrogen and the earth; and in-

deed it is only in this polar fashion that these oxyacid radicles, and many other radicles, may be said
to exist, for they are often incapable of any free
existence. With most metalloids oxygen forms
acids, for metalloids conduct heat slowly; hence
in intrametalloid combinations the heat discharges
tend more to be confined to the actors, and our
earth does not interfere to the same extent as when
there is metal or heat-transmitter in the action ;
hence the latent heat of the metalloid actors is,
in their mutual combinations, more shared than
given away to our earth, and the metalloidal
anhydrids come to be formed having a latent heat
higher than our earth's; and, as a rule, more
oxygen is used for acidifying the metalloids that
are latently cold and not of high heat capacity.
Oxygen further forms acids even with the lower
oxides of certain metals, as manganese, &c., for
such metallic oxides from their non-conductivity,
when producing by further oxidation metallic
acids, act like the latently colder metalloids. Such
metallic oxides do not conduct heat; hence in a
further combination with oxygen, the oxide takes
the fresh oxygen's heat to itself, and gives but
little to our earth; hence, by the addition of
enough of oxygen to these oxides, you gradually
increase the latent-heat mean of combination
until this mean becomes metalloidal and acid.

Hence it is not the oxides of the metals that
have lost earthward during their protoxidation the
most heat, such as the earth metals, that are the
most apt at forming with fresh oxygen metallic
acids; these metals become at their protoxidation
too negative to allow of facile heat discharges
between them and free oxygen, and are also the
most distant from the acid or metalloidal heat
mean. In an oxybase, which is a metallic protoxide, our earth, as it were, moved one chemical
step, by entering virtually into the mean of combination, in the direction of oxygen; and in an
oxyanhydrid, oxygen has come one stride down to
the earth by discharging some of oxygen's heat
into the other metalloids associated with the
oxygen in the anhydrid. In an oxyanhydrid the
ingredients have not gone far enough towards the
earth for the establishment of the just or equo-terro-
solar equilibrium; in an oxybase, the ingredients
have gone too far earthwards. But what is the
ultimate requisite for neutrality or chemical inactivity is, that the two chemical forces sun and
earth should have their equitable shares, or an
equilibric portion in the compound, and this
occurs finally when the oxybase and oxyacid
combine, forming an oxysalt. In an oxysalt,
earth, sun, metal, and metalloids are equo
balanced, and the oxysalt having not only the

special or mutual equilibrium, but a final one, or
one also with reference to the two great chemical
ever-acting forces, sun and earth, begins greatly
to lose all chemical activity, which want of complete, or of both internal and external, equilibrium
alone produces. This is expressed in chemistry by
saying that the acid and base neutralise each other,
destroy each other's chemical activity; and so they
certainly must do. In oxysalts, therefore, matter
has obtained a somewhat just share of sun power,
and on them dawns the aptitude for the assumption of beautiful forms. It is true that these
forms are, in the salts, as yet merely geometrical
or crystalline; but still even those humbler shapes
foreshadow to us the organised forms of life that
the gradual increase of sun-might, by means of
heat-fostering carbon in organic compounds, pro-
gressively develops; for facile crystallisation is a
great characteristic of salts. Again, when chlorine
unites, or rather equilibrises, with our earth,
through a suitable metal, the metallic chloride
resulting resembles an oxysalt, inasmuch as the
metallic chloride has neither too much of the
sun or earth; for chlorine is much less solar, or
latently hot and heat capacious, than is oxygen;
hence the heat discharges during the production
of metallic chlorides have not gone to such extremes as those of oxygen in the formation of

oxybases, and yet have passed quite beyond those
of the oxyanhydrids—that is, have gone pretty
much to the *juste milieu* of sun and earth or of a salt.
By the presence of hydrogen itself the hydracids
are formed. Hydrogen's position as an acid-producer is anomalous, and occurs, as we have seen,
because of hydrogen's great latent heat and capacity, but comparatively, for a metal, weak conductivity; so that the influence of our earth on
hydrogen does not drain away hydrogen's great
heat when hydrogen combines with certain elements, such as chlorine, that are distinctly latently
colder than hydrogen; hence the latent-heat
mean of combination of hydrogen with the halogens, &c., the hydrohalogenic acid, &c., is
isolated to the actors, and is not terrestrial, but
metalloidal, and greatly gaseous; and hence the
power of hydrogen or its heat to form acids with
such bodies. Again, hydrogen is much more heat
capacious and hotter than oxygen, being less hydro-
soluble; hence less of hydrogen will suffice to produce that positive or hot metalloidal mean called
acid than of oxygen; and we observe that the
hydracids have less of their acid-producer, hydrogen, than the oxyacids have of theirs, oxygen;
that is, we have oxyacids with seven equivalents
of oxygen, where generally one or more, rarely
two, or at most three, equivalents of hydrogen

suffice for an hydracid. In the other ingredients of hydracids, as iodine, sulphur, arsenic, &c., volatility and some lightness—that is, some of the attributes of heat capacity and of ready gaseous transformability—are essentials; for these substances are thus enabled to take with hydrogen a latent-heat mean of combination or form that must, from the circumstances of the case, be isolated or confined to them and hydrogen. Sulphur, because it is volatile, can, when combining with highly gaseous hydrogen, more readily meet it half way—that is, take the latent heat mean of combination, the midway form, with highly gaseous hydrogen—than if sulphur were not volatile; so that hydrogen, though a perfect acid-producer, is yet, being, so to speak, more exacting, not such an extensive or general one as oxygen. The metallic oxides that may serve as radicles of oxyacids, being incapable of assuming the hydrogenic isolated heat mean of combination, form no acid with hydrogen as they do with oxygen.

If we compare an oxyacid with a hydracid, we find that for hydracids there is no proper hydrate (Roscoe and Dittmar), and the hydracid (HCl) or hydrochloric acid is represented by one equivalent of chlorine and one of hydrogen (HCl). In this hydracid (HCl) the chlorine (Cl) represents the radicle of the oxyacid, such as that of sulphuric

acid (SO_3O); both the chlorine and the sulphuric
radicles are metalloidal solar chemicals seeking an
earth equilibrium, and taking it with oxybases,
and producing, for reasons already given, the
equo-terro-solar equilibrium termed saline. In
oxyacids the metalloidal part or radicle is compound (SO_3O); in hydracids it is elementary, and
generally a halogen (ClH), &c.; so that we have a
compound metalloidal chemical (SO_3O), the oxyacid radicle, acting just like a simple element,
metalloidal chlorine. But this is far from un-
usual, and we have compound cyanogen thus
acting; and the reason that cyanogen, which may
be held to be a radicle, can be isolated, is, that its
two ingredients, nitrogen and carbon, are, the first,
very latently hot, and the second cold, and the
two are thus well able to heat-balance each other;
whereas, in many other compound radicles, the
ingredients are not so constituted. The non-
isolability of many radicles is therefore no argument against their existence as polar ingredients
of compounds where they are equilibrised by our
earth or other good equilibric heat centres. The
halogens, &c., in hydracids, therefore, correspond
to and act the parts of the radicles in oxyacids,
and it is the hydrogen of the hydracids that
behaves very differently from that of the oxyacids.
Hydrogen in hydracids has no earth equilibrium,

and has to take it when it combines with a base; and hydrogen does this, and becomes water, or passes, when combining with the base ammonia, into what has been called the metal ammonium. The total action, therefore, of oxyacids and hydracids is not exactly alike, owing to the difference of the heat states and equilibrium of the hydrogen that enters into the composition of both. The oxyacid's hydrogen has an earth equilibrium; the hydracid's hydrogen has it not, but seeks it. If you add an oxyacid $(SO_3O)H$ to an oxybase, oxide of zinc (ZnO), the oxyacid radicle (SO_3O) passes from the water's hydrogen, which is a comparatively positive and worse earth equilibrium, to the oxide of zinc's zinc, which is a negative metal compared with hydrogen, and a better heat equilibrium for the positive sun elements (SO_3O) of the oxyacid radicle; and sulphate of zinc and water are produced $(SO_3O)H) + ZnO = (SO_4O)Zn) + HO$; that is, a stronger earth equilibrium, zinc, is substituted to the radicle, instead of the weaker one, hydrogen; and a salt, the sulphate of zinc, is produced, having an equal balance of earth, sun, and the chemicals concerned; a compromise, a neutralisation, a state of comparative repose, is reached by the ingredients of the salt, for they lose greatly the cause of chemical activity, which is non-equilibrium of latent heat with each other and surrounders.

If you add a hydracid to an oxybase, hydrochloric acid to oxide of zinc (HCl + ZnO), you
have the ingredients of the hydracid (Cl and H)
taking both the earth equilibrium that both seek,
the hydrogen (H) with the oxygen of the base as
water, and the chlorine (Cl) with the base's metal
as a metallic chloride (HCl + ZnO = HO + ClZn),
and the chloride resulting is, for reasons already
given, like the compounds or salts formed by the
radicles of oxyacids with metals. If you add an
oxyacid (SO$_3$O)H), sulphuric acid, to ammonia
(NH$_3$), the action is very different from that of
the common oxybases, for in ammonia there is no
oxygen at all, and the equivalent of oxygen
attached to the anhydrid of the oxyacid to form
its radicle (SO$_3$O) has not its fellow or correspondent in ammonia (NH$_3$), as it had in an oxybase (ZnO); on the contrary, it is nitrogen that
the equivalent of oxygen of the acid radicle encounters in ammonia (NH$_3$). Now, nitrogen is a
very latently hot metalloid, and exists in gaseous
ammonia (NH$_3$) in a very different state from
what oxygen does in solid bases; so that the two,
oxygen and nitrogen, are not exchangeable as
oxygen is exchangeable for oxygen in common
oxyacid and oxybasic combination. So that when
an oxyacid (SO$_3$O)H) combines with ammonia, we

L

have a new and very latently hot metalloid, nitrogen, not exchangeable with the oxygen of the
radicle, added to the action—we have, in fact, a
new acid radicle $(SO_2O)N$) produced; and the
presence of this very latently hot nitrogen in the
new radicle $(SO_3O)N$) necessitates a very free
earth connection in order to heat-balance it.
Hence the hydrogen of the oxyacid $(SO_3O)H$)
passes into terrestrial equilibrium, and we have a
salt formed, the sulphate of ammonia, in which
four equivalents of earth-bound hydrogen are required to be used, from the presence in the radicle
of the acid of nitrogen, and the sulphate of ammonia's formula is thus written $(SO_3O)N,HE_x$
$HE_xHE_xHE_x$. In the salt sulphate of ammonia
there is no compound metal at all, but only many
equivalents of the metal hydrogen, with a consequent large terrestrial copartnership or equilibrium. There is no need of the hypothesis of a
compound metal, seeing that hydrogen is itself
a metal: what is indeed necessary in the salt
sulphate of ammonia is not a new compound
metal (NH_4), but a compound acid radicle
(SO_3ON). Now, a compound metal, if it exists at
all, is unique in chemistry, whereas compound
radicles of the nature of SO_3ON are known to
abound. This acid radicle (SO_3ON) is the latently

hottest in chemistry, seeing that it contains nitrogen, and thus it requires a very extensive earth
connection to heat-balance it, and this large earth
connection can only be given by very heat-capacious
hydrogen; for by increasing the number of the
equivalents of hydrogen, you increase the earth
connection, but you do not, from hydrogen's great
heat capacity, much deteriorate heat capacity.
Four equivalents of hydrogen have the heat capacity inversely, as 4, and therefore are capable of
heat discharges, which depend on equivalents, and
which always occur in chemical action.   Hence
these four equivalents of hydrogen can act with
the very latently hot radicle SO_3ON, but no other
metal but heat-capacious hydrogen can; for if you
try to substitute four equivalents of hydrogen by
any other metal, you increase so much the equivalents as greatly to deteriorate capacity for heat or
for chemical action; for while the sum of four
equivalents of hydron is 4, the sum of four
equivalents of potassium is 110; so that this
radicle SO_3ON of the sulphate of ammonia cannot
form an analogous sulphate of potassium.   If you
add a hydracid, hydrochloric acid (HCl), to ammonia (NH_3), the action is quite similar to that of
an oxyacid; there is a new radicle formed (NCl),
also very latently hot from the presence of nitro-

gen, and thus requiring, in order to be balanced, four equivalents of earth-bound hydrogen; for example, $NCl, HE_xHE_xHE_xIIE_x$, chloride of ammonium.

PART II.

CHAPTER I.

Of the galvanic battery. The nature of the phenomena in a single isolated cell, and in many cells constituting a battery : the current traceable, after several removes, to our sun's heat, latent more or less in all things : the current of a single and of a combination of cells : reason of the augmentation of tension by addition of cells : electrolysis, its nature.

In order to commence the study of galvanism, let us take a galvanic cell, reduced to its simplest. Let us immerse a potassium and a platinum plate in distilled water, without allowing them to touch under the water, and, on the contrary, connect the two plates outside the water by a wire. In such a cell we have the means of producing a powerful galvanic current in a way that is yet convenient and uncomplicated, and suited to initiatory reasoning. In the above-mentioned cell the electromotive force is the oxidising potassium. Let us, therefore, first of all, confine ourselves to this oxidation, and take altogether away the platinum plate from our cell. During the protoxidation of potassium in the protoxides of hydrogen or water

of this cell, we have two things concerned—a free
metal potassium and a protoxidised metal, hydrogen.
But a protoxidised metal means a metal that has
a terrestrial form or latent heat or equilibrium, a
metal, namely, that has got latently earth cold by
the discharge or disoccupation of its latent heat,
by burning with oxygen, a metal that has no
longer a position of advantage over our earth, but
that, in fact, represents our earth herself; and such,
therefore, is the hydrogen of the water of our galvanic cell. Potassium that is immersed in that
water being, however, free, has a form or latent
heat not like our earth at all, but rather a form
that potassium obtained in furnaces whose heat is
finally traceable to the sun, and which therefore
represent the sun; so that free potassium has a
sun form, and has thus a position of advantage
over our earth,—a necessity or power, by the
potassic heat constitution, of rushing into equilibrium with her or with her latent heat or her
form, by discharging latent heat into herself, or
into any of her representatives. So this potassium
being free and possessing conductivity, and a furnace
or sun or positive or latently hot form, thrown under
water, comes into contact with the water's hydrogen,
that is latently earth cold or negative, and that represents our earth, and latently hot potassium is
forced to discharge heat into this latently cold hydro-

gen, and to assume a terric equilibrium by protoxidation with the water's oxygen.   In the decomposition
of water by potassium there is a struggle for the
terrestrial equilibrium between two metals free, solar
potassium and water's terrestrial hydrogen, and
the potential that is in latently hot free solar
potassium enables it to conquer or displace the
hydrogen, that has only earthly force or potential;
that is, latently hot potassium has enough of heat
in itself, together with the power of discharging
it, to displace the earth-negative hydrogen from
its terrestrial equilibrium in water, and to evolve
it as gas—that is, potassium decomposes water.
And the surfaces of potassium thus decomposing
water, or burning or oxidising in water's oxygen,
solidifying oxygen, discharging heat, moving into
terric equilibrium, disoccupying potential, are
always covered with bubbles of the water's hydrogen, that is, deoxidising, gaining latent heat or
potential, moving away from terric equilibrium,
or passing from a terric to a solar form, from
liquidity to gaseity : the said hydrogen gains what
the said potassium loses, motion, potential, heat,
solar equilibrium.   Nothing is lost or created in
this potassic water decomposition; the potassic
energy, heat, obtained ultimately from the sun,
the earth-equilibrised water's hydrogen, when
evolved, took and stored up or potentialised, to

give up at any time if burnt. The force that
drove the particles of negative earth representing
water's hydrogen from the terric to the solar
equilibrium was the converse movement of the
molecules of solar potassium from its solar to a
terric equilibrium. On the part of potassium and
oxygen there was solidification, that is correlated
to our earth and negativeness; at the opposite pole,
or on the part of hydrogen, there was the vaporisation that is correlated to our sun or positiveness. The heat that boiled the liquid hydrogen
of the water into gas was given by the correlated
burning of the potassium with the oxygen of the
same water; hence from the burning potassium
decomposing water there is a current of heat into
the boiling hydrogen that is evolved from the
surfaces of the potassium; and this is important, for this current is the galvanic one *in initio.*
Hydrogen exists allotropically as a liquid in its
water combination; to raise this liquid to a gas,
during the decomposition of water, must require
heat, and this is furnished by the combination or
oxidation of potassium, that exists in the closest
propinquity to the hydrogen. The burning potassium boils the liquid hydrogen on its surface.
Potassium and oxygen thus discharge heat into
the water's hydrogen, because that hydrogen is
latently earth cold, and the potassium furnace or

sun latently hot; because the hydrogen is the
latently coldest object with which the heat-discharging potassium and oxygen are in contact;
and because that hydrogen represents our earth,
and the heat discharge is the galvanic current in
embryo. But hydrogen in its water combination
or allotropy is not a very latently cold object,
being only a liquid; further, hydrogen, during
the decomposition of water, transforms greatly
from liquidity to gaseity, so that the discharge
of heat from the potassium into the hydrogen,
during the decomposition of water, is none of
the easiest; for hydrogen is not latently cold
enough urgently to constrain this heat discharge; and the great transformation of hydrogen
is yet another difficulty to the ready acceptance of
heat; so that hydrogen, though it represents the
earth, does so badly, worse than any other metal
does. If we connect by wire, therefore, the potassium, in the act of decomposing water, in the act
of discharging heat into this hydrogen, with a
metal that is much latently colder, much better at
conducting heat, and quite passive, with platinum,
in short, we then offer to the heat discharged from
potassium a far better earth-representative than was
the hydrogen into which the potassium was previ-
ously heat-discharging, and consequently the heat
will pass first into the latently colder untransform-

ing platinum, where it finds the least resistance,
before finally discharging into the hydrogen; so
that by the presence of platinum, and its connection
by wire with the potassium in the galvanic cell we
study, we facilitate heat-discharge, and by so doing
encourage chemical action; and we must divert
the heat current from directly passing from the
potassium into the hydrogen, by making it go
first to the platinum; and if we observe the platinum that is connected by wire with the potassium
in our completed galvanic cell, we find that it is
covered with the bubbles of hydrogen, which
proves that that which alone can evolve the hydrogen as gas, the potassio combustion-heat, has left
the potassium, and passed along the wire to the
platinum, from the surface of which the liquid
hydrogen is now boiling and escaping as gas.
But still the heat that is evolving liquid hydrogen
as gas is the heat of the potassic combustion, for
the platinum upon which this hydrogenic evolution
occurs is perfectly chemically inactive, and hence
there is no other source of heat in the galvanic
cell but the burning potassium. Potassium in
this way connected with platinum in this cell
seems to cease to burn, and the platinum it is that
seems to be burning; and, quite analogously,
hydrogen oxidising in the presence of platinum
seems also to cease to burn, while the platinum it

is that then gets red hot. After the addition of
the platinum to our cell, the heat or the galvanic
current still remains the same—the same in origin
and destination, the same in causation and effect,
produced by the potassic combustion, and expended
in the vaporisation of a liquid, the hydrogen. The
only important difference is, that the current has
been diverted round by a wire first to the platinum
plate, instead of passing direct from potassium
giving to the hydrogen receiving it. To reach the
platinum, the heat produced at potassium has only
one course, namely, the connecting wire, for the
cell's water that lies between the potassium and
platinum plates does not conduct heat, and along
this wire the heat may be seen going. When,
therefore, there is platinum present, connected by
wire with the potassium in a galvanic cell, there
is no longer discharge of heat from potassium
giving directly to the hydrogen taking the heat,
but the heat current is forced to take a circuit
round by the wire, and first to the colder and untransforming conductive platinum, when the heat
finally passes into the hydrogen, which it evolves
as gas, and heat equilibrium is thus completely
restored and established. In this single galvanic
cell, therefore, the potassium is negative, because
it is losing latent heat; the platinum is plus or
positive, because it takes this potassic heat; and,

finally, the hydrogen gets also positive with the
cell's water it pervades, for hydrogen it is that
finally occupies the heat. There is a heat current,
not through the non-conductive water of the cell,
but along the wire connecting potassium and
platinum outside the cell, and this current goes
from the potassium, where it originates, to the platinum where it is equilibrised by discharge into
the hydrogen. The platinum becomes positive just
because it was negative before the action, while
potassium becomes negative because it was before
the action positive to our earth; and the whole
action results from the necessity of equilibration of heat, sun-heat with earth-heat. But there
is no current through the water of the cell, seeing
the water does not conduct it. What occurs in
the water of the cell is not a transmission of the
current, as current, through it, but a correlated
polarisation of the water's ingredients, hydrogen
and oxygen, by the effects of the current. Water
is a metallic protoxide, composed of the metal
hydrogen and of oxygen; of these two ingredients,
the metal hydrogen is the most negative to the
earth of the two, or most connected with our
earth, for, as an oxide, hydrogen cannot get lower
in heat relations with our earth, and is as like
our earth as hydrogen can, as an oxide, be; but
oxygen's form or latent heat in water is not as

like our earth's as it can be, for there are many
metallic oxides, as lime, in which oxygen reaches
solid infusibility ; so that of these two ingredients
of water, oxygen and hydrogen, the oyygen is still
positive to our earth, or more so than the hydrogen, though between the two ingredients themselves there is perfect neutralisation or similarity
of latent heat or equilibrium. Into this so constituted water two metals are plunged—potassium constantly discharging latent heat, and the platinum
constantly receiving this heat, that is, potassium
permanently earth negative and the platinum positive as to latent heat. In these circumstances, the
positive oxygen of the water will be repelled from
the positive platinum and attracted by the negative
potassium, and this repulsion and attraction will be
reciprocal and mutual, so that oxygen will be
urged to the potassium by a fourfold force ; and the
negative hydrogen of the water will be repelled
from the negative potassium, and attracted by the
positive platinum, and these attractions and repulsions will also be reciprocal and fourfold. As
soon as the liquid hydrogen of the water, urged
by these fourfold attracting and repelling forces,
reaches the platinum plate, the heat that the liquid
hydrogen finds there, coming along the wire from
the burning potassium, is discharged into the liquid
hydrogen, which evolves it as gas ; as soon also as

the liquid oxygen of the water, urged also by the
fourfold attracting and repelling forces, reaches the
potassium plate, the two combine, burn, solidify,
discharge heat, which passes along the wire to the
platinum to meet the hydrogen, and the potassium
and oxygen assume a terrestrial solid negative
form or equilibrium, the opposite to the solar or
gaseous positive form that the hydrogen assumed
at the opposite extremity of the cell. Not the
current as current, but its influence, correlated
attraction, magnetism, polarisation of the water's
ingredients, exists in the cell. Something does
occur in the water of the cell, therefore, but it
cannot be the passage of a current of electricity
of low tension, as such, through it, but it is the
polarisation of the ingredients of the water of the
cell. Let very carefully distilled, cold, airless water
be chosen, and let two pure new platinum electrodes
be put into it, and connected with the single cell
we are studying, which consists also of distilled
water and wire-connected potassium and platinum
plates immersed in it, there will result not the
slightest effect on the distilled water with the platinum electrodes by a current coming from our said
cell. In both cells there is distilled water; in the
one containing potassium and platinum, the water,
according to the present theory, conducts electricity perfectly; in the other, containing only plati-

num electrodes, not at all, although the electricity is
the same and the water is the same. The reason is
very difficult to see or find if you hold the present
theory, but very clear if you observe that the current in the water of our cell is not the electric
current as such, but its polarising effects on the
water's ingredients, which effects fail to occur if
both electrodes used be platinum and unoxidisable,
or only then occur when one of the platinum electrodes becomes itself polarised by the induction of
a many-celled battery; which polarising effects
on water's ingredients, however, appear naturally
when oxidising and non-oxidising plates or electrodes are used. The potassium and platinum plates
being plunged in distilled water, the instant that
the two are metallically connected above the water
a strong current passes; that is, according to the
present theory, positive electricity passes through
the water from the potassium to the platinum, and
from the platinum through the wire above the
water back to the potassium, and the circuit is said
to be completed. If this were true, the distilled
water of the cell must be as good a conductor of the
electricity as the wire above it, for the very instant
of contact the whole round of wire and water is
said to be completed by the galvanic electricity;
hence its current must have passed as freely and
quickly through the water as the wire above

it. But it is allowed by electricians themselves
that water's galvanic electric conduction is
many million times worse than wire's. How is
it possible, then, that water and wire can, under
any circumstances, conduct that electricity exactly
alike ? With profound deference to the many great
minds that have so held or so hold, it must be
said that it cannot be, that the phenomena of the
galvanic cell cannot be thus logically interpreted.
Water is a liquid protoxide of a metal, hydrogen.
In the ingredients of this water, therefore, in its
oxygen and hydrogen, there exists already an earth
polarity ; for we have found that all metals during
their protoxidations are thrown into latent-heat relations with our earth, and attract our earth. Of
the ingredients of water, oxygen is more positive
to our earth than hydrogen, for oxygen can as an
oxide become much more solid than oxygen exists
in water ; hence the ingredients of water, oxygen
and hydrogen, are like a suspended magnet, earth-
swung, with a negative pole—hydrogen turned to
the earth's equator and a positive pole, oxygen
turned to the earth's pole. But the hydrogen and
oxygen, as ingredients of water, do not attract
each other, being only in equilibrium, and are
therefore quite free to move round each other ;
and in so moving they do not alter in aspect
nor decompose, for to do either they must get

latent heat; but the potassium and platinum plates,
with their connecting wire, plunged into the water,
constitute, the moment the current passes, another
magnet, which is fixed, the positive pole of which
is the platinum plate, and the negative the potas-
. sium. We have, therefore, a latent heat magnet
—the potasso-platinal—brought beside one free
to move, namely, the water's ingredients, the oxy-
hydric one ; and of course the instant the potasso-
platinal fixed magnet is plunged into the water
or placed in relations with the oxyhydro-movable
magnet of water's ingredients, the two magnets
react on each other, and the ingredients of water
forsake their earth polarity, and swing round into
a magnetic position with reference to the nearer
potasso-platinal magnet ; that is, the negative
hydrogen of the water points to the positive platinal plate, and the positive oxygen to the negative
potassic pole or plate of the potasso-platinal magnet. All these movements must occur consenta-
neously, and almost synchronously, and can only
occur in fluids whose particles are free to move.
These phenomena in the water in the galvanic cell
in action, therefore, consist in a mere change of
its ingredients' polarity from the earth to the zinco-
platinal polarity or magnet, and are not visible. We
know by experiment that potassium in burning
discharges a certain amount of heat, which has even
M

been measured. We know that the electro-motive
force in metals is as their heat-giving powers when
oxidising or metalloidising; we know that a liquid
cannot be boiled without heat; and we know that
in the galvanic cell we study potassium oxidises or
burns, and that liquid hydrogen is boiled; that
these two phenomena occur *pari passu* and synchronously, and according to the specific heats of
the boiler and the boiled,—the boiling of the hydrogen must be connected with the burning of the
potassium. The one explains the other, and without the one there is no satisfactory explanation of
the other. Hence the galvanic current is one of
the latent phases of heat passing essentially from
the potassium to the hydrogen—from one substance representing positive to another representing negative; or, if you choose, from a latently
hot to a latently colder, or from our sun to our
earth, or, as we shall hereafter see, a current
or transference of molecular or atomic motion
from the rapidly pulsating potassium and oxygen
to the hydrogen. When there is nothing but the
potassium and water concerned, the potassium
decomposing water, solidifying with oxygen, discharges its combustion heat directly into the
water's hydrogen, and we see the water's liquid
hydrogen boiling on the surface of the burning
potassium, for hydrogen is then the latently coldest

object with which heat-discharging potassium is
in contact. But when platinum is at the same
time in contact with the heat-discharging potassium, we have a much latently colder object than
water's hydrogen presented to the heat; further,
this new object, platinum, conducts heat and is
passive. Viewing, then, heat as a force, it is clear
that heat will find less resistance in the direction
of the platinum, and thus will pass there, and thus
eventually reach the hydrogen—and to do so, the
heat goes round by the wire, for from the fluid
or water of the cell the heat encounters insur-
mountable resistance; and thus we get a heat
current on the wire passing from the burning
potassium, first, to the passive platinum, and
eventually to the boiling hydrogen, and so carried
away, and heat equilibrium for all actors reached.
In the galvanic cell which we study, and merely
to simplify reasoning, we chose the metal potassium as the electro-motor, but it is evident
that any other solar, or latently hot, or positive,
or earth-equilibrium-seeking metal, which means
oxidisable metal, the more the better, might have
answered as well, since the essential for the production of a galvanic current for the present may
be held as sun-heat passing under certain disguises
or phases in the direction of the earth. We also
chose platinum for the other galvanic metal, but

it is also manifest that any other metal that
better represents our earth than water's hydrogen,
that is, a metal that is latently cold, negative, and untransforming, the more the better,
might serve.   We chose water, but it is clear
that any other metalloidal compound capable of
giving and taking to, and with a metal seeking
it, a terrestrial equilibrium, might do.   For we
repeat, that the essential to the production of
galvanic currents is the passage into terrestrial
equilibrium of sun-heat that is latent in certain
chemicals, generally a metal and metalloid; sun-heat
equilibrising with the general or preponderating heat
state of our earth matter.   This passage of sun-
heat into the earth we can by certain contrivances
make to occur along a wire, where we can utilise
and study it in several ways.   That metal, therefore, is the best electro-motor that is the most
solar, that is nearest to liquidity and gaseity, that
has the most sun-got latent heat, that is thus the
most unlike our earth, and that consequently has
the most necessity, urgency, to become like her,
that has the highest position of advantage or
potential over her; in these consists a metal's
electro-motive force.   For the metal, therefore,
that is to be our electro-motor in our battery, we
chose one that is likest, so to speak, the sun
matter; but for the other metal, the non-electro-

motor, we chose one that is just the reverse, one
that is most like our earth's typical matter ; and
the more perfectly the non-electro-motor represents
our earth, the more will it suit the other, or solar
or electro-motor galvanic metal, for there will be
between them greater necessity of heat exchange
or balance. But our typical earth is solid, latently
cold, untransforming ; hence the non-electro-motor
metal of a galvanic battery ought to be so likewise. To give rise to a galvanic current, we must
have a metal that has latent heat, that is, a metal
that is near liquidity or gaseity, that is fusible and
volatile ; that is essential, but not that alone ; for
to give rise to a galvanic current, a metal must
not alone have latent heat, but must also discharge it ; but the power of heat discharge in a
metal does not always correspond with the metal's
quantity of latent heat, for reasons somewhat
difficult to trace. Thus a metal, mercury, has
considerable latent heat but very inferior heat
capacity, as seen by its great weight and equivalent, so that mercury cannot readily give out
its latent heat. It has great electro-motive power,
but cannot put it forth. It is, as it were, a strong
man bound. That mercury has good electro-
motive powers, under favouring circumstances, we
have, however, ample proofs, for all amalgams are
better electro-motors than their simple metals.

Mercury, to combine with potassium into an amalgam, both being conductive metals, must take the
isolated latent heat mean of chemical combination,
that is, latently colder solid potassium will share
in amalgam part of the latently hotter liquid,
mercury's heat, and in potassic amalgam we
have a potassium that is latently hotter than free
potassium; hence, as electro-motive force in a
metal is the amount of latent heat and the powers
of its discharge, we shall have that force greater
in amalgamated than in free potassium. Amalgamated potassium has both more latent heat to
discharge and more urgency to discharge it, while
the potassium conductivity and equivalent are
deteriorated only so far as slightly to impede
action. And what is true of potassium amalgam
is true for other amalgams. In this galvanic cell
we are studying, we observed first that the protoxidation of the metal potassium is the electro-
motive force, but this electro-motive force is not
inherent in potassium, but has come to it ultimately
from the sun, and it is only certain heat relations
and endowments of potassium that make it a fit
receptacle and vehicle for this sun energy. The
ultimate electro-motive force, therefore, is produced
by the action and reaction of our sun and earth,
and is one of the ways that sun-heat passes
chemically into the earth. Great powers are

therefore concerned in these apparently isolated galvanic actions, and astonishing results are therefore to be remarked And it is easy to perceive how our sun comes to represent always the positive force and our earth the negative. There are metals that represent our sun; these metals are positive, their forms tend to fluidity and gaseity, and if they be at the same time light and heat-capacious they are also good electro-motors, because there is then a possibility of discharge of their latent heat earthward, and when this happens these positive metals become of course earth negative. If these sun metals be heavy and little heat capacious, as is mercury, there is still a possibility of their becoming, in peculiar circumstances, electro-motors, but under usual states their latent heat or galvanic electricity is imprisoned in them by the difficulty they have of rapidly discharging it.

There are metals, on the contrary, that represent our earth; they are negative, their forms tend to great or infusible solidity; they are heavy and little heat capacious; heat in them tends to do the smallest amount of work, and appears in these metals as amorphigenic heat or temperature, and these metals have the passivity of our earth. The heat relations of these negative metals to our earth are quite different from those of the positive

metals. The negative metals represent themselves heat centres of equilibrium, and are much
more able to take a morphigenic heat than from
their own resources to give it; and these metals
often possess in action an obvious advantage over
the mere earth, because they are as passive as conductive, and can be brought near to the actors.
Hence we see platinum in certain chemical actions
taking the heat unto itself that otherwise ought
to have gone to our earth; as in the combinations of gaseous hydrogen and oxygen, where we
see hydrogen cease to burn or cease to discharge
heat into our earth in order to discharge it upon
the platinum, which becomes by the reception of
this heat red-hot. Hence we see the platinum
plate in the galvanic cell taking the heat of the
burning or oxidising potassium plate, and thus
prevailing there over the hydrogen and our earth
equilibrium which that hydrogen badly represents.
Hence the metals that best occupy platinum's
position in a battery are latently cold (not very
fusible), are passive, untransformable, little heat
capacious; they thus receive heat as temperature
without exacting work from it. Hence we find
that the more compact, that is, untransforming
sorts of carbon, the latently coldest of the elements, will readily take platinum's place in a
battery. Carbon is indeed a little earth, and a

magnificent centre of heat equilibrium, but of a
transforming equilibrium, and its usual forms are
too morphigenic to suit well galvanic purposes
where passiveness as well as latent coldness are
required.

Galvanic electricity is therefore nothing else but
sun energy that has assumed a peculiar phase in
oxygen or metalloid and metal. When there is nothing but solar metal and solar oxygen and our
earth acting, we say the first two burn, for we
then see their sun-got latent heat, which is incompatible with a terrestrial form, leave the two
as they take that form, and as the heat leaves
them without doing in that act any work of permanent transformation, we see it as heat.

When a solar metal burns in the oxygen of
water, the solar metal takes also its oxide or
earth-like form, and as surely discharges the heat
incompatible with that form; but then this heat
we do not see as heat, for it does permanent work
in transforming the water's liquid hydrogen into
gas or any other oxidised metal to a solar or free
form. To see this heat as heat, we must burn
back the hydrogen reduced or gasified by potassium
decomposing water, and then we see well enough
the heat that was in potassium-evolved-hydrogen.
The heat of burning potassium decomposing water
passes into our earth or hydrogen, because both

are latently cold, and the heat will pass into
platinum or its like in preference to our earth or
hydrogen if platinum be present, and if the platinum be connected by wire with the potassium, for
platinum has the advantage over even our earth
herself, that platinum is in actual contact with
the actors.   There is, therefore, nothing inexplicable thus far in this generally called galvanic
current; it is a sun-heat current.   We see this
in the current's acknowledged origin, a burning
metal,—in its course along the wire, which the current can make red-hot,—in the current's termina-
tion, a boiling liquid, water's hydrogen.   The
reason of the current's origin is that it springs
from a portion of the earth, a metal and metalloid,
—that the sun or its representative, fire, is capable
of overheating, of heating out of proportion to the
heat of the surrounding great mass of matter of
which the majority of the earth consists.   The
sudden cooling of these overheated bits of the
earth, the metal and metalloid, is the origin of
the current, and the cooling occurs by a passage of
the heat potentially tensified right into our earth,
or into any portion of latently cold matter with
which the overheated portions of the earth comes
into close chemical contact.   Such is the origin of
the current, its destination may be gathered from
its origin, for a body that has been overheated

will part with ·its heat not to objects as hot as
itself, but to those that are colder. Hence the
heat's passage to both platinum and hydrogen, pre-
ferring platinum, for both platinum and water's
hydrogen are negative, are earth latently cold, platinum free by its inherent nature, and hydrogen
by protoxidation. Platinum being greatly negative or latently cold, and hydrogen much less so,
the heat goes by preference first to platinum, and
only then passes into hydrogen; and the heat from
burning potassium can only reach platinum and
hydrogen by the wire, for the fluid of the cell does
not conduct this heat, and on this wire the heat
is always demonstrable as heat. The current cannot pass through the fluid of the cell; it is impossible, as the fluid does not conduct it; but the
current polarises the ingredients of the water or
of the cell fluid; and even this is explicable on
the supposition of its being a latent heat current.
We see that a metal that is burning in air or discharging heat is always attracting oxygen, and
the reason, we have seen, is, that the metal is
then in connection with our latently cold negative earth, and can thus readily get earth
cold, the metal is negative, latently cold, by
help of our earth, and thus attracts powerfully the very positive or latently hot, since
highly gaseous, oxygen. When, on the contrary,

a metal in its oxide state gets reduced, it gets
heat discharged into it, and therefore becomes
latently heat positive, as in the heated red oxide of
mercury, and the metal then repels its oxygen,
since the two separate; that is, a metal losing
latent heat and negative attracts oxygen, a metal
gaining latent heat or positive repels oxygen.
The same thing happens in the cell of a galvanic
battery where a metal is burning or oxidising, not
indeed in air, but in water; and these attractions
and repulsions are doubled or quadrupled by reci-
procity. Most of the phenomena, both chemical
and galvanic, of a single simple voltaic cell are
therefore quite intelligible by considering that we
have to do with a current of latent, morphigenic heat
got from our sun—far more intelligible, it seems to
me, than by holding the current to be we know not
what, or by holding that the current in a single cell
has the complete characters of friction electricity,
which assuredly the current of a single cell does
not possess, and acquires, for reasons presently to
be considered, after the addition of several cells.
Whatever be the true theory of galvanism, the
present one is untenable; not alone because it
explains little of galvanic phenomena, but because
it is obliged to hold that the fluid of the cell and
wire conduct the current exactly alike, which, beyond the slightest doubt, is false.

In the simplest form of a galvanic cell we
observe, as the action proceeds, that the platinum
becomes coated with a film of minute bubbles
of gaseous hydrogen—that is, with a solar and
highly positive metal, where a terrestrial and a
negative metal alone ought to be. This persis-
tent presence of a highly positive metal, gaseous
hydrogen on platinum, impedes the further transference of heat from that platinum to the rest
of the hydrogen still liquid, and does not call,
as it were, the positive current in that direction,
as a negative metal would. On the contrary, the
presence of this positive metal — free gaseous
hydrogen on the platinum—tends to induce on platinum a negative state, and to originate a current
from the hydrogen back to the potassium, hence
the action of the battery is much impeded.
This has been ingeniously evaded by Grove,
by roughening the surface of the platinum,
by which the gaseous hydrogen is at once
cast off, and also by Daniel, by suppressing
the hydrogen altogether by the reduction in its
stead of copper. In the galvanic cell we study,
therefore, we have a burning metal, potassium, or
more usually zinc, discharging heat in the presence and heat connection of two other bodies,
hydrogen and platinum ; transforming latently hot
hydrogen, bad at receiving heat, and platinum,

passive and latently cold, and good at receiving
heat; hence the heat goes first to platinum before
going to the hydrogen. It is, in fact, just because
this hydrogen is a metal that has to transform
greatly in the actions of the galvanic battery, and
that in its earth-like or oxide shape is the latently
hottest of all metals, that heat does not readily
affect hydrogen, and that we can get in the galvanic battery the heat destined for hydrogen to
go round by the wire to a metal platinum that is
very passive and latently cold; that, in short, we
can get a good galvanic battery at all. Hence,
when potassium or zinc reduces any other metal
but hydrogen, say lead, in the transformations of
which, from a state of oxidity to metallicity, from
its earth form to its sun form, less heat work is
expended than when hydrogen is reduced, seeing
the difference of latent heat between free and
oxide lead is smaller than between free and oxide
hydrogen. Zinc, then, always discharges heat
directly into the lead, even if we then connect the
heat discharging zinc with platinum, for the lead
in its oxide is very negative, and in contact with
the zinc, and has, by thus being in contact with
the heat source, the advantage over a platinum
plate, which is separated by the distance of the
wire; and the heat in the reduction of the lead by
zinc does not take the circuitous route by wire to

the platinum, but goes directly from the reducing
zinc to the reduced lead; and from such a combination as zinc in a lead solution, though we
certainly get galvanic electricity, yet we get no
galvanic battery. We also get no battery from
the chemical actions of solutions of some of the
metalloids—the halogens upon metals. These
chemical actions are certainly violent, and as certainly electric, but the electricity or heat produced
passes directly into our earth, for it is our earth
herself that is in this case concerned, and not a
bad representative of her, as is hydrogen in the
galvanic battery; we therefore cannot readily
divert the earthward heat current, and thus get
no battery. We have thus passed in review the
galvanic and chemical phenomena of a simple voltaic cell.

What is the nature of the current? It is one
of a phase of sun-heat passing into an equilibrium,
generally into our earth, or something that represents her; the current is thus demonstrable, as
heat and light with a solar spectrum. The current
will pass into what best represents our earth, into
the most negative object with which the current is
in good heat communication. In the galvanic cell
we studied, this is first platinum, then hydrogen.
The current originates in burning potassium, thence
it passes by the wire to the platinum, and from

the platinum it passes into the hydrogen brought
by attraction molecularly into contact with the
platinum ; by the hydrogen, the heat is occupied
and carried away, equilibrised. A current of latent
heat passing into our earth, as we remarked when
studying chemical action, always polarises the
earth, and is polarised by it ; that is, will assume
what are called magnetic relations with the earth ;
that is, will turn to or choose or attract by preference the earth's latently coldest portion, or her
magnetic pole ; hence the latent heat current in
the galvanic battery will also polarise the fluid of
the cell that represents the earth in miniature, and
attracts and is discharged into that fluid's latently
coldest ingredient into its negative pole, that is,
the hydrogen, to which the positive current has
an attraction, which the negative hydrogen reciprocates.   In the fluid of the cell, though there
is, properly speaking, no current, there is its
correlated magnetism and chemical transformations ; and there being no current in the cell
through the fluid, the direction of the current in
the wire must be not from the platinum plate to
the zinc, but the reverse, from the zinc to the platinum ; for a current must start from the place whence
it originated.   And we have even ocular proof that
the current passes from the zinc to the platinum ;
for in the case of the charcoal points, in what is

called the voltaic arc, it is that charcoal point
connected with the burning zinc plate or pole of
the battery, and that, therefore, by our proposed
theory, first gets the heat that first becomes white-
hot. If the incandescence of the charcoal point
is an effect of the passage of the current, which
surely none doubt, where incandescence first
occurs, there the current first passed. Again,
just as a bit of charcoal gets hollowed out by receiving the heat current or blast from a common
mouth blowpipe, the so-called positive, but really
negative, charcoal point becomes hollowed out by
the current of heat our proposed theory holds is
being discharged into it. Again, if we watch carbon's general behaviour in chemistry, we find it
a negative element, highly capable, or, so to speak,
attractive, of the positive equilibrium or forms;
this is also seen in the charcoal points, for it is to
the so-called negative, but really positive, charcoal point that the polarised particles of charcoal
are mostly transported. The transportation of
matter from voltaic arcs of various material will
vary according to their ingredients.

Let now any number of galvanic cells, say four,
such as that we have been studying (A, B, C, D),
as seen in diagram, be connected by four wires
(E, F, G, Q), the zinc plate in the cell A with
the platinum plate of its neighbour at B by the

N

wire E, and the zinc plate in the cell B with
the platinum plate in the cell C by the wire F,
and the zinc plate of the cell C to the platinum
plate of the cell D by the wire G, and the zinc
plate of the cell D with the platinum plate of the
cell A by the wire Q, so that the zinc and
platinum in the same cell do not touch, but are

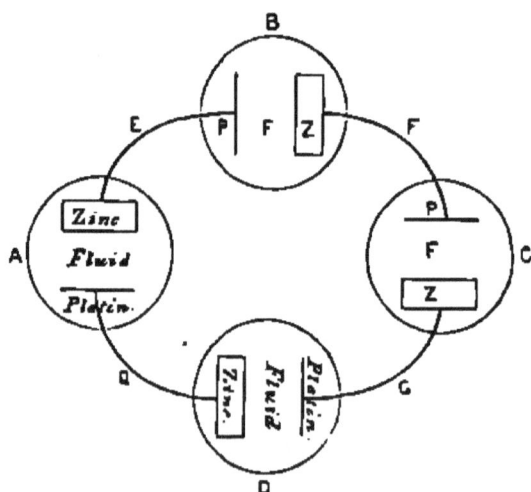

separated by the oxidising fluid of the cell, but
the zinc and platinum of neighbouring cells touch,
or are connected by the wires E, F, G, Q; then
the heat of combustion that must be discharged
by the oxidising zinc will be 5° in the direction of
least resistance, that is, into the latently coldest
most conductive passive object with which heat-

discharging zinc is in free heat communication.
To zinc oxidising in air, this object is our earth;
to zinc oxidising singly in a weak acid, this
object is earth equilibrised or earth representing hydrogen; to zinc oxidising in a weak acid,
in good wire communication with latently cold
untransforming metals, such as platinum and its
congeners, the primary object of discharge is
platinum or similar metals. The heat of combustion therefore discharged by the zinc of the
cell A, taking the direction of least resistance,
passes along the wire E to the platinum plate of
the cell B, and there evolves the hydrogen, and
is completely equilibrised and escapes; but this
hydrogen evolved in the cell B was alone furnished
by the correlated oxidation of the zinc of the cell
B, and thus this zinc of the cell B is forced to
oxidise just as the heat coming from the zinc of
the cell A will allow it.   But the heat of the
burning zinc in the cell B passes along the wire
F to the platinum in the cell C, where the heat
evolves the hydrogen, and is completely occupied
and equilibrised; from the cell C the heat of the
burning zinc goes through the wire G, and does
the same in the cell D as in the other cells.
Hence it arises that the heat that vaporises
hydrogen in any of the cells comes from a neighbouring cell; and thus a system of checks is esta-

blished between every cell of a battery, one cell necessarily checking its neighbour; indeed a single cell checking or influencing the chemical phenomena in all the cells of which even the largest battery may be composed; so 'that, if we substitute any of the cells by a weaker one, by one having smaller plates or weaker ingredients, all the other cells necessarily come down to the level of the weakest cell, and we greatly injure the power of the battery. This is what by our proposed theory must inevitably occur, and does so; but what explanation of this fact does the present theory give? From the concatenation of the cells of a battery, as held by our proposed theory, all the chemical actions going on in all the cells must be equivalently quite alike, and the heat travelling along any single wire that connects to neighbouring cells, say the wire F, must be equal in quantity to the heat passing along any other single connecting wire, say G or Q; for the heat on each of these wires, by our proposed theory, has perfectly equal causation and effect; that is, the heat on all the wires has been produced by the oxidation of chemical equivalents of zinc, and evolves equivalents of hydrogen; hence the amount of galvanic electricity found passing round in any part of the circuit at the same time is equal in every vertical section of

the circuit. What explanation does the present
theory give of this? By our proposed theory it
also strictly follows that we cannot increase the
quantity of the heat or galvanic electricity of a
battery by the addition of cells, seeing that by
our proposed theory the current is limited to two
neighbouring cells, originating in the zinc of the
one and terminating completely in the platinum
and hydrogen of the neighbouring cell with which
the current has a wire connection. The current
therefore does not exist as a through current along
all the cells from one end of the battery to the
other, as the present existing theory holds. If
it did, the current of a first cell passing into a
second cell would there be reinforced by the current of the second cell, and would be, on issuing
from the second cell, doubled, or at least would not
be exactly equal to the current of the single first cell.
How can a through-and-through current, after
the addition of five hundred cells, remain exactly
the same in quantity as the current of a single
cell? Again, we know that although we do not
increase the quantity of the current of the battery
by the addition of cells, yet we thus augment its
tension; and the meaning of this word *tension* is,
that you develop by induction in this current,
which, limited to a single cell, is but a current
of sun-got latent heat, the polarity proper to

electricity; that is, you make what is negative or
positive in the current in a single cell more negative or positive by the addition of cells, hence
you increase the necessity for, and with that the
power of irruptive discharge between negative and
positive currents or their polarity; and the current's
identity with electricity begins to appear. For
we have just seen that, in the single galvanic cell
that we carefully studied, we have, in fact, perfect
latent heat analogues of two magnets, the zinco-
platinal or fixed magnet, and the suspended mobile
magnet, the earth-swung ingredients of the fluid of
the cell, oxygen and hydrogen, or the radicle of an
acid and hydrogen. The positive pole of the fixed
magnet is at the platinum plate, and that of the
mobile one at the oxygen or radicle of the acid;
the poles of the two magnets, the fixed and
movable, when the current passes in our single
cell, must each at once get turned and attracted
to the one of opposite denomination in the other
magnet, and by their induction they tensify the
powers of each other. In a single cell we have
two magnets concerned and four poles, each by
induction acting and reacting upon each other,
and all these poles mutually strengthen each other,
as the guard is known to improve and sustain the
magnetism of a common magnet : and as with the
addition of each cell to a battery two other magnets and four poles, all acting inductively in the

proper direction, accrue to the battery, each negative pole becomes more and more negative, and
each positive pole more and more positive, with the
addition of cells, and the necessity of the discharge of electricity between the poles increases,
and the tension, power of disruptive discharge,
or polarity characteristic of electricity, augments
also. It is, therefore, the very fact that the current,
as current, is confined to the wire, and only exists
in the fluid of the cell as magnetic polarity; that
you can tensify the current by increase of cells,
otherwise you would merely increase its quantity.
By the present theory the view of the current's
course through a number of cells does not explain
the production of tension, and is, besides, full of
anomalies, and indeed of contradictions; for the
current is said to start from the positive platinum,
and to pass along the connecting wire to the
negative zinc of the neighbouring cell, then
through the fluid of that cell to the positive
platinum in that cell, and then again along a
connecting wire to the negative zinc of another
neighbouring cell, and so on; that is, a current
going first through good metallic conductors, then
through fluids, the worst conductors, with like
ease; a current first going from positive to negative, then from negative to positive, and that
through the fluid, the very worst of conductors.

Why should electricity in the fluid of the galvanic
battery be held to go from negative to positive,
and that through the worst of conductors, when
electricity elsewhere is never known to do so, even
in the very best conductors?

The substances decomposing or decomposable by
galvanism are called electrolytes; the decomposition itself, electrolysis; and the extremities of the
two wires plunged opposite each other into the
electrolyte, and that come, one wire from the zinc
and the other from the platinum plate of a battery,
and that are thus said to carry the electric current into the electrolyte, are called electrodes. The
only way of viewing electrolysis is to consider the
electrolyte, with its fluid and its two opposite
electrodes, as but another cell that has been added
to a battery. The electrolyte itself corresponds to
the fluid of a cell, and the two electrodes correspond to the two plates of a proper galvanic cell;
for the electrodes, even when both are made from
the same metal, say platinum, are subjected to the
inductions of all the virtual latent-heat magnets
of which we have seen that a galvanic battery in
action consists, and thus the two electrodes come
to be, the one negative and the other positive,
although made of the same material; and this is
proved by taking them rapidly away from the
battery, and testing them immediately by a gal-

vanoscope. This electric difference of even platinum electrodes has been called the polarisation of the electrodes; and, in the detached polarised electrodes, the current must pass from that electrode which corresponds to a zinc plate to that which corresponds to a platinum one. That the actions going on in an electrolyte fluid are strictly analogous to those of a proper galvanic cell is proved by the fact that it is electrolytes alone that can produce electricity, even in the proper galvanic cell, and *vice versa;* and it is because of this necessary analogy of electrolytic with the proper galvanic action of the cell fluid that galvano-chemical decompositions or electrolyses are limited in number and variety; it is not because these galvanically indecomposable liquids do not conduct electricity that they are not decomposed by it; it is because the chemical acts and constitution of those indecomposable liquids have no analogy, no correspondence with the chemical acts that originate galvanism. Those indecomposable liquids cannot approximate enough in action to galvanic cells; and liquids exist which conduct galvanic electricity without decomposition.

Even an electrolyte with two platinum electrodes is, therefore, a species of galvanic cell, but always an imperfect one; for one of those two platinum electrodes has, in forming a galvanic cell, to

become negative, has to discharge heat, or to originate a galvanic or latent-heat current; bnl the
electrode being of platinnm, is highly, intrinsically
negative or latently cold, non-transforming, chemically inactive, and cannot readily do so, even with
the great assistance of the induction of the whole
cells of the battery. If such an electrolyte contain
ingredients with very slight possibility of action
upon platinnm, as chlorine, then the platinnm
electrode that has to become negative does so by
being attacked by, and by combining with, the
chlorine ; for the induction of the whole battery is
forcing and helping the electrode to a negativeness obtainable by such a chlorine combination,
just as, contrariwise, a conversely analogous induction will prevent copper in a battery from being
oxidised or attacked at all. With pure and cold
water, and two platinum electrodes, it becomes
very difficult to form an electrolyte—that is, a
galvanic cell—since the oxygen of the water not
having any possibility of action with platinum,
platinum cannot get negative by oxidation, and
has to become negative by the shear pressure of the
number of cells or of magnets of multiple batteries
brought to induct upon it. It is different with
the so-called electrolysis of water acidulated with
sulphuric acid ; for it is the sulphuric acid, which
consists, as we have seen, of a radicle (SO_4O) and

of hydrogen, that is decomposed, and not the water
itself. Of sulphuric acid, hydrogen (H) is the earth-
negative ingredient or pole, and the radicle (SO_2O)
the positive. The radicle and hydrogen are ingredients of a compound, and therefore not attracting, but only in equilibrium, and free to move
round each other without decomposition, for which
heat is necessary; and in an electrolytic cell the
negative hydrogen of this acid will be attracted
to the positive pole or electrode—that, namely,
that is zinc-connected, and that has received heat
along the wire from the burning zinc plate of the
battery. The positive radicle of the acid will be
attracted to the negative electrode—that, namely,
that is connected with the platinum plate of a
battery. In electrolysis, when the acid's radicle
(SO_2O), which is a liquid, gets to the platinum-connected or negative electrode, the positive liquid
radicle (SO_2O) discharges latent heat upon the
negative electrode by then losing one equivalent
of oxygen, and becoming the solid anhydrid SO_2.
Part of this heat received by the negative electrode
from the liquid radicle as it changes into solid
anhydrid evolves generally as ozone, one equivalent of oxygen, and the rest of the heat passes on
to the battery to keep up its heat actions, and
the solid anhydrid formed is instantly hydrated
and liquefied by the surrounding water. The

negative hydrogen of the electrolysed sulphuric
acid is attracted by the positive electrode, which
is wire-connected with the heat-discharging
burning zinc of the battery, and thus this electrode is latently hot and positive, and by its heat
the hydrogen is evolved as gas; so that it is the
molecule of water that is combined with the sulphuric anhydrid that is in reality decomposed,
and not the pure water.   A platinum electrode
may originate a current, therefore, with very great
difficulty, by mere pressure of powerful and
multiple inductions from many-celled batteries,
or this electrode may of course originate a current if it aptly transform chemically, and in this
it is assisted by the inductions aforesaid; or the
platinum electrode that has to become negative
originates currents, even if assisted by adequate
chemical transformations, not in itself, but near it,
in the ingredients of electrolytes, as we saw occurring in the electrolysis of weak sulphuric acid, or by
having the electrode's surface covered with chemicals, by the combinations of which heat-discharging actions can occur, as shown by Schönbein, &c.
When an electrode metalloidises or acts chemically,
then its electrolyte is a galvanic cell to all intents
and purposes.

The polarity of electrolysis results, in fact, as

we have tried to elucidate, from the law of chemical combinations, from the dualistic nature of these
combinations, and depends entirely on the latent-
heat states of the two electrodes. We have seen
that the zinc-connected electrode is the latently
hot one, for it receives along the wire the heat discharged by the burning zinc of the battery ; the platinum-connected electrode is the latently cold one,
for its heat is sent through the connecting wire to
the platinum of a battery. These two latently negative and positive electrodes will always attract their
latent heat opposite. The metals and bases, which
we found to be latently cold or negative, will be attracted to the latently hot or positive pole, that is
wire-connected with the burning zinc of a battery ;
the metalloids and acid radicles, which we found
latently hot or positive, will be attracted by the
negative electrode, that connected with the platinum of a battery, to which this electrode must discharge heat, and thus become negatively related.
By our proposed theory, the current being reversed,
the denomination of the poles are reversed also.
No chemical transformation can take place without heat ; hence decompositions can only occur at
the electrodes, for in one of them alone the heat
necessary for these transformations is found,
and in the other it is developed. The acid of an

electrolysed salt is attracted to the negative or
platinum-connected pole of a battery, to the pole
that has no latent heat, because the acid in a
salt is the positive ingredient; and this acid in
its ingredient state, going to the electrode, may
pass through blue solutions without reddening
them, because the acid, in its ingredient state,
is allotropic, transformed, neutralised by certain
latent-heat changes occurring at combination, and
these require to be reversed before the ingredient
acid can return to its free condition, and these heat-
changes can only, as a general rule, as we have just
seen, be effected at one of the electrodes.

But it sometimes happens that, in the electrolysis of a salt, its acid, passing through certain
solutions, may obtain heat of transformations even
before reaching an electrode.   In the electrolysis
of a tartaric acid salt, the acid, before it reaches the
proper electrode, gets no heat, and is thus allotropic with the neutralised properties that acids as
ingredients of salts must have; and such an acid
cannot redden blue.   If such an acid, however, by
electrolytic attracting polarities, be made to pass
through a solution of sulphate of silver, it decomposes that sulphate of silver, and forms an insoluble tartrate of silver; for here the passage of the
soluble oxide of silver of the sulphate of silver into

insolubility, as the silver tartrate, gives the latent heat necessary for the transformation of the allotropic tartaric acid into the free or true acid; a heat effect independent of the electrodes.

CHAPTER II.

Short view of the dynamical theory of heat, as applicable to the
ideas of this work.

WITH regard to the dynamical theory of heat, we
at once see the utility of the views brought forward
in this work, for by them we at last obtain the
action and reaction necessary for the continuous
molecular motion of matter assumed by that theory;
for the ultimate particles of matter are subject
constantly to the antagonistic forces of our sun
and earth.   Let us take the smallest conceivable
or ultimate particle of any element, say potassium.
This single ultimate particle of potassium, though
so small as to be invisible to the sight and microscope, yet possesses the same heat constitution as
the largest piece of potassium; for on matter itself,
and not on its physical pores, must depend its
heat constitution.   The potassic particle, then, will
contain a certain amount of matter, and will have
the capacities for the three degrees of latent heat
and great elasticity; hence the potassic atom will
have its peculiar power of giving and taking latent

heat in its three degrees; the particle will have
the power of fully adapting itself to heat or cold,
to positive and negative. Upon the particle so
constituted are acting in nature two very great
forces, our sun and our earth, that represent our
sun-heat or positiveness, and our earth-coldness
or negativeness; so that we have the potassic particle constantly latently heated by our sun and
cooled by our earth down to her own special heat
level. But latent heat is correlated to form, so
that the potassic particle latently heated by our
sun, and so also cooled by our earth, is likewise
dilated by our sun and contracted by our earth;
hence the potassic particle is as a little heart, constantly pulsating, throbbing, dilating and contracting to our sun and earth; the diastole
being given by our sun, and the systole by our
earth, and the two constitute a potassic particle's
throb or pulsation. These throbs succeed one
another with great rapidity, for there is an almost
continuous stream of sun-heat from our sun,
through, as it were, the potassic particle into our
earth, and thence partly back into space. From
the quickness of the succession of the particle's
throbs, we should not see them at all as throbs,
even with a microscope of sufficient power to perceive the particle itself, nor could we feel these
pulsations even if we could handle the particle;

o

for all our physical senses can receive only a blur or uniform impression from the pulsating particle, just as in a musical note we hear what seems a continuous sound, though in truth the note is composed of many quickly succeeding pulses. Our sun and earth's action on the potassic particle is consentaneous and direct; the way for the passage earthward of sun-heat through the particle is prepared and clear; the passing heat is not diverted nor impeded by surrounding particles, for they have also their equitable share, have as much as they can take, of sun-heat; hence this heating and cooling, or dilatation and contraction, or motion or throbs, of the potassic particle are rapid, for they are the unobstructed direct result of two great and universally acting forces, our sun and earth. The potassic particle's throbs (force *vive*) occur, therefore, because of the presence of our sun and earth, and of a heat constitution in the particle having a dualistic susceptibility for heat and cold, and also because of the correlation of latent heat to matter's dilatation. Hence analogous throbs must exist in the particles of every chemical throughout nature, and these particles all pulsate synchronously. But in every chemical the throbs will have different sizes, seeing that the heat constitution upon which the throb depends differs in

every chemical. The throbs will vary in size even
in the same chemical if the virtual distances of
sun and earth forces, part of the throb-causers, be
varied, as by fire or virtual sun approach, or by
cold or sun recession, or earth's preponderance
or virtual approach, or also if the throbs of surrounding matter be varied as by pressure or re-
laxation, &c. When the potassic particle dilates,
all the matter in it must expand equally and
synchronously, for the matter is homogeneous,
and acting under the same dilating cause; and
the expanded particle will thus retain its shape
and mass. This mass has, of course, a relation to
the relative weight of potassium, and this shape
has probably a likeness to that of a potassic
crystal. But as the volume of the expanded
potassic particle is increased, the specific gravity
decreases. Upon the size of the potassic atom's
throb, therefore, will in a measure depend the
specific gravity of the potassic matter. Under usual
circumstances the potassic throb-size will not vary,
for our sun cannot over-heat or over-dilate the
potassic throb-size, for our earth, acting by her
own and through potassium's heat constitution,
resists. Nor can our earth over-cool or over-con-
tract the potassic throb-size, for our sun through
the potassic-heat constitution will not allow it;
hence the potassic throb-size, under usual circum-

stances, remains the same, and has during expansion enough of density of matter in it to give the
resistance and coherence called solidity. But if
we increase the expansion of the potassic particle's
throb, we rarify its matter, and this may reach such
an extent as to make the particle's matter offer little
resistance to our touch or to the effects of pressure
of the surrounding pulsating atoms, and then the
particle will become liquid or even gaseous, if
the matter in the particle be sufficiently expanded
and rarified during the particle's pulsation. If, on
the contrary, we contract the size of the potassic
throb, we densify its matter, and tend to produce
greater and greater solidity of its particles, thus
diminishing motion or force *vice;* for the matter
of the throbbing particle is eminently elastic, and
as capable of dilatation as of contraction. If we
put our throbbing potassic particle into an ima-
ginary hydraulic press, we can reduce the space
around the particle by pressing power, and the
particle in such a press will have to throb according as the diminished space around will allow,
and will thus have, while pressed, a throb of less
size, and heat will be correlatively disoccupied
in the contractedly throbbing particle; and the
potassic particle in a press will exist over-cooled
with regard to the usual terro-solar equilibrium;
and the pressure of the press, by coercing the sun

force, alone gives to the particle the possibility of this unnatural existence; for pressure tending to produce contraction is a coadjuvant of our earth in her struggle with the sun's or expanding force. The moment the press is taken away, the particle will return to its natural latent heat state or dilatation, any other existence being impossible to the particle, heat constituted as it is; and to regain its pristine heat, the particle takes heat from its surroundings, or cools or contracts them. We find, therefore, that mechanical pressure or contracting power can substitute and coadjuvate earth force in balancing sun force or heat expansive power, and we see how this can be, since both pressure and earth force tend to contract matter or still motion; hence we obtain some theoretical clue to the mechanical equivalent of heat. But if the potassic particle's throb be amenable to the pressure of a press, it must also be affected by the pulsating atoms of things around. All particles, of all bodies, pulsate round potassium with a synchronous dilatation and contraction, and they all, during dilatation, hem each other in, according to the size, rapidity, and force of their throb. When two chemicals, such as oxygen and nitrogen, that have greatly the three latent heats, and consequently very widely dilated, synchronous, and nearly equal pulsation, are close

together, as in the atmosphere, the pressure of
surrounding throbs upon two special particles
cannot force them any nearer each other; that is,
oxygen and nitrogen do not molecularly, chemically, attract each other. But when we bring carbon close to oxygen, then there are two particles,
the oxygenic and the carbonic, that have very
unequal latent heat. The carbonic particle, being
very latently cold, has a very small-sized throb,
and the oxygenic particle a large one; and this
inequality of the pulsations between carbon and
oxygen makes room between their molecules. A
want of resistance to pressure there, and the
pressure of surrounding pulsations, force the two
carbonic and oxygenic particles together, and keep
them so. The two particles are said to attract
each other, but it is not exactly so; they are rather
forced together by the pressure of the pulsations
of all things; hence the power of molecular attraction is often immense; hence we see why
attracting chemicals must be in different states
of latent heat, which means, in an inequality of
pulsation or motion. Again, if a particle's
throbs be amenable to great pressure, they are
also affected, of course, in decreasing ratio, by
lesser pressure; and it is not difficult to conceive
how hammering, paddling, rubbing, may modify
the throb-size of particles, so as to produce in

the same substance increase or decrease of throb-
size and disoccupied heat, or the reverse, and, by
friction between two different substances, a polar
difference or phase of heat, known as electricity;
for, when two pieces of the same substance are
rubbed together, their particles' throbs having
the same properties, are contracted or dilated
alike in the two substances, and we only get disoccupied heat, and no polarity or difference of
effect, known as positive and negative electricity.
But when two different substances are rubbed,
then their particles, being of different nature
and properties as to elasticity, &c., are affected
unequally, and in the one substance the pulses are
contracted or become negative, and in the other
are dilated or become positive; and when we say
contract, we also include diminution of movement
or of force *vive* in the matter of the particle; for
all throbs, great and small, being synchronous, the
matter of the widely throbbing or latently heated
or positive particle has to move much faster than
the less widely throbbing or latently cooled or
negative particle. The phenomena of induction
are also deducible from these views. If a set of
particles be throbbing less than natural, that is,
negatively, then the elastic particles in immediate
neighbourhood get room to throb wider or posi-
tively, and do so; hence in nature you cannot have

a positive without a negative, and *vice versa;* and
the positive and negative will be always pushed
together by surrounding pulsations, or will attract
each other. We see in the earth, from her relations to our sun, that her ultimate particles must
be pulsating very unequally; the pulsations of the
equatorial terrestrial matter are much wider than
the polar; hence, perhaps, one reason for the greater
length of the diameter of the earth through the
equator. If we place a solenoid, the matter of
which is throbbing unequally, largely towards the
platinum plate, contractedly towards the zinc, then
the solenoid, if free to move, will assume a position in which its throbs will meet with least resistance from surrounding throbs; the solenoid
will assume a magnetic position; and we have
only to suppose that a steel magnet composed of
very negative carbon and much more positive iron
has a polarity of throbs, to see that that magnet
also should behave as the solenoid. In the neighbourhood of strong electro-magnets, therefore, the
throbs in surrounding particles in the air and other
matter may be influenced, may be made to beat
slower or quicker, and this is found actually to
be the case. Indeed, it may be that particles of
the same substance cohere or remain together
greatly because of the equality of their own
throbs, and the pressure of the others surrounding

them. Again, in these views we get some hint
of the cause of the upheaval of the earth's strata,
and the increase of terrestrial temperature with
depth, and to the origin of volcanic fire, and
even to certain phenomena of vegetation; for
terrestrial particles, the more they exist towards
the earth's centre, the more are they subject to
pressure of surrounding matter; and so pressed
do the deeper particles become, that the dilating
effect of heat on them can barely or not at all
occur, and the heat that reaches them from our
sun must be greatly thermometric, and round the
deeper terrestrial particles there exists therefore
less heat latent, aud more thermometrical. But,
nevertheless, there exists in these deeper particles
of the earth a constant tendency to dilate, which
on any slight reduction of pressure above them
may occur, producing earthquakes and even volcanic action. By careful development of the
study of these relations of the particles of matter
to our sun and earth, it seems to me that we may
attain a hope, a possibility of comprehending
a little more distinctly the correlation of the
forces of nature called heat, electricity, magnetism, and chemical affinity to each other,
and of understanding their phenomena in detail.
Even the establishment of such a hope, or

even the attempt at it, may do good ; and to the last I trust I can lay claim, and to the martyrdom that assuredly awaits the obscure and isolated preacher of new doctrine.

THE END.